Classical Subjects Creatively Taught

GREEK ALPHABET CODE CRACKER

Get your secret Code Cracker support files at this website:
www.ClassicalAcademicPress.com/greekcode
Username: codecracker
Password: iliad

Dr. Christopher Perrin

Classical Academic Press • Camp Hill, Pennsylvania
www.ClassicalAcademicPress.com

Greek Alphabet Code Cracker

Version 1.0

ISBN: 1-60051-035-3
EAN: 9781600510359

Cover art by Rob Baddorf
Interior design by David Gustafson

Classical Academic Press
3920 Market Street
Camp Hill, PA 17011

www.ClassicalAcademicPress.com

Table of Contents

Introduction to Teachers:

You have made a bold decision to teach your students Greek. We congratulate you!

Greek is a beautiful and fascinating language that has enriched the minds of countless people over the centuries. It is the basis for much of the technical terminology in both science and medicine and is responsible for about twenty percent of the words in our English vocabulary. Learning Greek is also the gateway to reading and studying the New Testament as well as the writings of scores of classic Greek authors, from Homer to Aristotle.

Amazingly, children are not the least bit afraid of Greek and its intriguing sounds and curious letters. While adults tend to be intimidated by learning a novel alphabet, and a line of Greek words can look to them like an undecipherable code, that is not so with children. They will be happy, indeed, to "crack the code" of the Greek alphabet.

Knowing that children like adventure stories and secret codes, in this book we have cast the students in the role of detectives who, by learning to decipher Greek-rendered clues, will solve a dastardly crime. Students will love learning the Greek alphabet, even as they enjoy working as sleuths. If you are new to Greek as well, you will be able to learn right along with your students.

The book is divided into eight chapters and can be reasonably completed in eight weeks if you spend three to four periods per week using the text. Some teachers may want to slow the pace down or speed it up, depending on the age and ability of their students. It is better to do a little bit regularly than to schedule rare but long classes. In other words, four sessions a week at twenty minutes per session is far better than one class of eighty minutes!

The book proceeds gradually, adding six new Greek letters at a time. Students may need more help with assignments (especially with the Robbery Witness reports) during the first three chapters than they will need as they progress into later chapters. Therefore, it would be wise to plan to give more time to the first three chapters of the book. Also, it will help students immensely if you regularly sing and chant through the Greek alphabet, having the students look at each letter as they sing. An audio file of the Greek Alphabet Song has been provided on our website to help you and your students sing through the alphabet. We recommend that you begin and end each session with this song.

Please be sure to consult the other online resources that are available at www.classicalacademicpress.com/greekcode. You will find other audio recordings for use with the text, along with additional exercises and worksheets.

We think that your students will greatly enjoy this journey through the Greek alphabet, so be prepared for them to soon be clamoring to study *Song School Greek* or *Greek for Children*.

Sincerely,

Christopher A. Perrin

Christopher A. Perrin, Ph.D.
Greek Detective

Mission Briefing:
The Greek Urn Caper

Urn of Achilles

Welcome, Detective. You have quite a tough job ahead of you. Yesterday, the Grecian Urn of Achilles was stolen from the Cityburg Museum, and we need you to get it back. There are several suspects in custody (see page 6), but they aren't talking, so you must use the clues given to us by witnesses to discover the identity of the thief and recover the stolen urn.

In order to crack the case, however, you'll need to learn the Greek alphabet, which we use to encode important information. This book will teach you all that you need to know to crack the Greek alphabet code (or cypher) and solve the crime. Along the way, you'll find lots of fun exercises and challenging puzzles to help you sharpen your skills and increase your knowledge. In no time you'll become a full-fledged Greek Alphabet Code Cracker, ready to solve this case. Once you have discovered the name of the criminal and where he or she has taken the urn, you can go on to use your skills in all sorts of exciting ways, including sending secret messages to your friends!

Well, you better get started—there's a lot to do, and I'm sure you're eager to begin. Good luck!

Sincerely,

John Q Hoover

John Q. Hoover
Senior Code Cracker

CRIMINAL SUSPECTS
6' 5"
6' 0"
5' 5"
5' 0"
4' 5"
4' 0"
3' 5"
3' 0"
FISH-LIPS LOUIE
Runs an illegal gambling outfit across state borders.
MR. MINI
Robs banks by holding a stick of dynamite. Wanted in nine states.
RUBY-RED REBECCA
Has stolen over $1 million in European rubies.
DR. PETRI DICHE
Attempting to clone his own army of lab rabbits to take over the world.
FLORENCE THE FORGER
Prints counterfeit money to support her expensive tastes. Sought after by Interpol.

UNIT 1

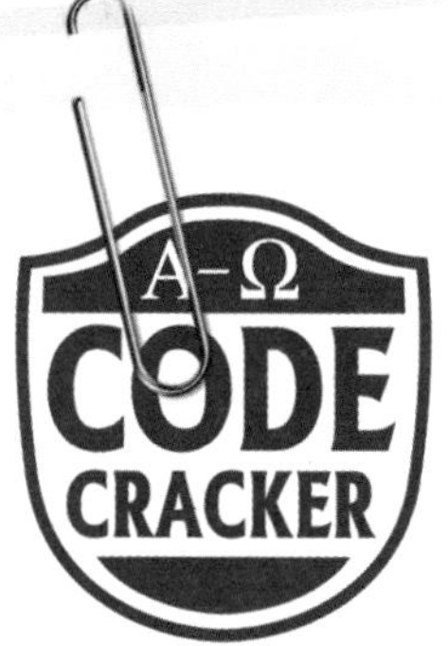

Mission Briefing:
The Greek Alphabet

Just look at the Greek alphabet over there on the Cypher Card! Doesn't it seem exciting? It's curvy and squiggly, but still friendly. It's strange in some ways, but still familiar. If you look carefully, you will see that nearly half of the Greek alphabet has carried over into English. That means that if you know your English alphabet well, then you already know about half of the Greek alphabet!

Look at the first two letters of the Greek alphabet. Have you seen them before? What do they look like? That is right, they look like an **a** and a **b** from the English alphabet. These two letters have come from the Greek alphabet right into the English alphabet. Guess what the names of these two Greek letters are. The first is called **alpha**, and it makes the same sound our **a** makes. The second letter is called **beta** and it makes the same sound our **b** makes.

Now say **alpha** and **beta** together quickly—**alpha-beta**. What word does that sound like? Exactly! We get the word **alphabet** from these two Greek letters.

This book is going to teach you how to "crack the code" of the Greek alphabet. Soon, you will be able to make the sounds for each of the twenty-four Greek letters and then make and read words using them. If you learn your Greek letters, you will be able to write in a code that only students of Greek can read—a secret code. As you go through this book, you will use this code to solve puzzles and to discover who is behind the theft of the Grecian Urn of Achilles. You will become a Greek-reading detective!

Robbery Witness Reports

Below is the first of several witness reports that will help you to narrow down the identity of the thief. As you go through the book, be sure to read each of these reports carefully. In each report you will find several words written using the Greek alphabet code. On a piece of scrap paper, change the red Greek letters to English letters, using the Code Cracker Cypher Wheel from the back of the book and any other tools you may need to help you. Then, using the rest of the report as your guide, determine what the proper English words are and write them in the spaces provided. We've decoded the first one for you.

Note that when you are translating between Greek and English, the number of letters used may be different. For instance, you'll notice that the first word we have written in Greek letters is ρερ, which translates to **rare** in English.

Once you've cracked the code in each report, use the facts provided to eliminate one of the suspects (you can see the lineup on page 6). **Use a pen or marker to cross them out as you go.** Once you have cracked the first four clues, you should have narrowed down the list of suspects until the real thief is uncovered.

Good luck!

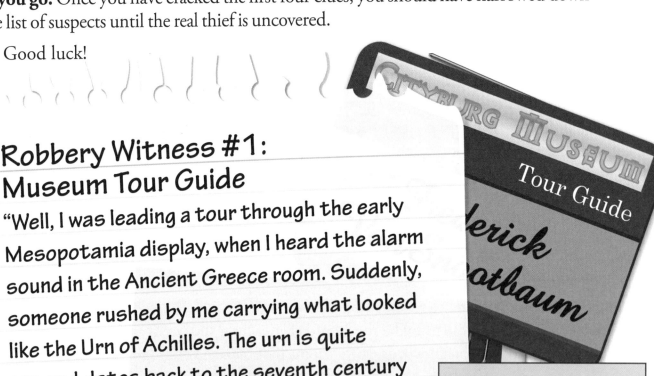

Robbery Witness #1: Museum Tour Guide

"Well, I was leading a tour through the early Mesopotamia display, when I heard the alarm sound in the Ancient Greece room. Suddenly, someone rushed by me carrying what looked like the Urn of Achilles. The urn is quite ρερ and dates back to the seventh century BC. It was donated in the year AD 1983 by the deceased widow, Ms. Werthenmuch. The thief moved very φαστ, so I didn't get a good look, but I noticed the suspect was wearing some sort of hατ.

English Words:

#1: r a r e

#2: ___ ___ ___ ___

#3: h ___ ___

Here is the Greek alphabet! Sing the Greek Alphabet Song using the audio files available online (www.classicalacademicpress.com/greekcode), making sure to look at each letter as you sing it. You may even want to point to it with your pencil or finger as you sing.

Upper Case	Lower Case	Name	Sound
Α	α	Alpha	/a/ as in **father**
Β	β	Beta	/b/ as in **boy**
Γ	γ	Gamma	/g/ as in **got**
Δ	δ	Delta	/d/ as in **dog**
Ε	ε	Epsilon	/e/ as in **get**
Ζ	ζ	Zeta	/dz/ as in **cords**
Η	η	Eta	/ay/ as in **rake**
Θ	θ	Theta	/th/ as in **thistle**
Ι	ι	Iota	/i/ as in **pit**; /ee/ as in **ski**
Κ	κ	Kappa	/k/ as in **kite**
Λ	λ	Lambda	/l/ as in **lime**
Μ	μ	Mu	/m/ as in **math**
Ν	ν	Nu	/n/ as in **nose**
Ξ	ξ	Xi	/x/ as in **oxen**
Ο	ο	Omicron	/o/ or /aw/ as in **offer**
Π	π	Pi	/p/ as in **pistol**
Ρ	ρ	Rho	/r/ as in **rat**
Σ	σ,ς*	Sigma	/s/ as in **soup**
Τ	τ	Tau	/t/ as in **tea**
Υ	υ	Upsilon	/oo/ as in **hoop**
Φ	φ	Phi	/ph/ as in **phone**
Χ	χ	Chi	German /ch/ as in **Bach**
Ψ	ψ	Psi	/ps/ as in **oops**
Ω	ω	Omega	/ō/ as in **note**

*Sigma has two forms—**σ** and **ς**. The latter is called a final form and is only used when it is the final letter in a word.

Now try the Greek Alphabet Sound-Off. Your teacher will lead you through this sound-off, or you can follow along with the audio file. Notice that every time you say the letter you are also making the sound that letter makes!

Greek Alphabet Sound-Off

Ah-, ah-, alpha—*ah-, ah-, alpha*; b-, b-, beta—*b-, b-, beta*;
g-, g-, gamma—*g-, g-, gamma*; d-, d-, delta—*d-, d-, delta*;
eh-, eh-, epsilon—*eh-, eh-, epsilon*; dz-, dz-, zeta—*dz-, dz-, zeta*;
ay-, ay-, eta—*ay-, ay-, eta*; th-, th-, theta—*th-, th-, theta*;
ih-, ih-, iota—*ih-, ih-, iota*; k-, k-, kappa—*k-, k-, kappa*;
l-, l-, lambda—*l-, l-, lambda*; m-, m-, mu—*m-, m-, mu*;
n-, n-, nu—*n-, n-, nu*; ks-, ks-, xi—*ks-, ks-, xi*;
aw-, aw-, omicron—*aw-, aw-, omicron*; p-, p-, pi—*p-, p-, pi*;
r-, r-, rho—*r-, r-, rho*; s-, s-, sigma—*s-, s-, sigma*;
t-, t-, tau—*t-, t-, tau*; oo-, oo-, upsilon—*oo-, oo-, upsilon*;
f-, f-, phi—*f-, f-, phi*; k-, k-, chi—*k-, k-, chi*;
ps-, ps-, psi—*ps-, ps-, psi*; oh-, oh-, omega—*oh-, oh-, omega*.

NOVEMBER 2007

Art MONTHLY

THIS ISSUE: HOW TO TELL A POLLOCK FROM A DROP CLOTH

Robbery Witness #2: Art Critic

"I was studying intently the use of κολορ and light in the paintings of the great Renaissance artists, when a most rude individual carrying a large vase of some sort knocked me down. At the time, I had assumed the person was simply a careless museum worker relocating the item. The piece was rather dull and certainly not as lovely as the color palettes of the fine fourteenth-century masterpieces. I had no idea it was of such value. Oh, right, you asked about the θιφ. I am fairly certain that they were not wearing any γλασσες."

English Words:

#1: ___ ___ ___ ___ ___

#2: ___ ___ ___ ___ ___

#3: ___ ___ ___ ___ ___ ___ ___

UNIT 2

Mission Briefing:

The First Six Letters

Using the first six letters of the Greek alphabet, you can start making secret code words. First, though, you must be sure that you know the sound that each letter makes. Can you sing through the alphabet song and the sound-off from memory? Can you make the sound of each of the letters? If so, you are ready to start building words! Note that the Greek letter **γ** is not a **y**! It makes a **g** sound, not a **y** sound.

Draw a line to match each Greek letter with its name:

Delta	ε
Zeta	γ
Alpha	β
Gamma	δ
Epsilon	ζ
Beta	α

Now see if you can match the name of the letter to its corresponding capital (uppercase) Greek letter by drawing a line between them:

Delta	**Α**
Zeta	**Ε**
Alpha	**Γ**
Gamma	**Δ**
Epsilon	**Β**
Beta	**Ζ**

Circle the English letter that makes the same sound as the Greek letter at the beginning of each row:

Training Exercise

α	e	i	a	o
β	p	b	d	g
γ	d	y	g	u
δ	a	o	d	b
ε	f	e	c	o
ζ	z	y	c	g
Α	H	A	V	T
Β	D	R	B	P
Γ	G	T	F	E
Δ	V	A	Y	D
Ε	F	E	H	T
Ζ	S	T	Z	Y

Robbery Witness #3: First Grade Student

"Yeah, I was dragged to the museum on one of our boring field trips. The rest of my class was looking at boring paintings of one bowl of fruit after another. I was looking at the modern art section because I thought it looked much more fun. My mom has some of my art hanging on the fridge and I think it looks a lot like that stuff. Still, I was getting bored again, so when I saw this grown-up carrying some old ποτ, I asked what ταιμ* it was because I saw that they were wearing a ταιμπις* on their wrist. I didn't notice anything else."

*In Greek, the letters "αι" together make the long "i" sound.

English Words:

#1: ___ ___ ___

#2: ___ ___ ___ ___

#3: ___ ___ ___ ___-___ ___ ___ ___ ___

Now it's time to practice writing your Greek letters. First, trace the letters provided, then write the letter on your own in the blank space provided. As you write each letter, be sure to say out loud the sound it makes. Before you start, recite the Greek alphabet sound-off, using the audio file if you would like.

Cypher Practice

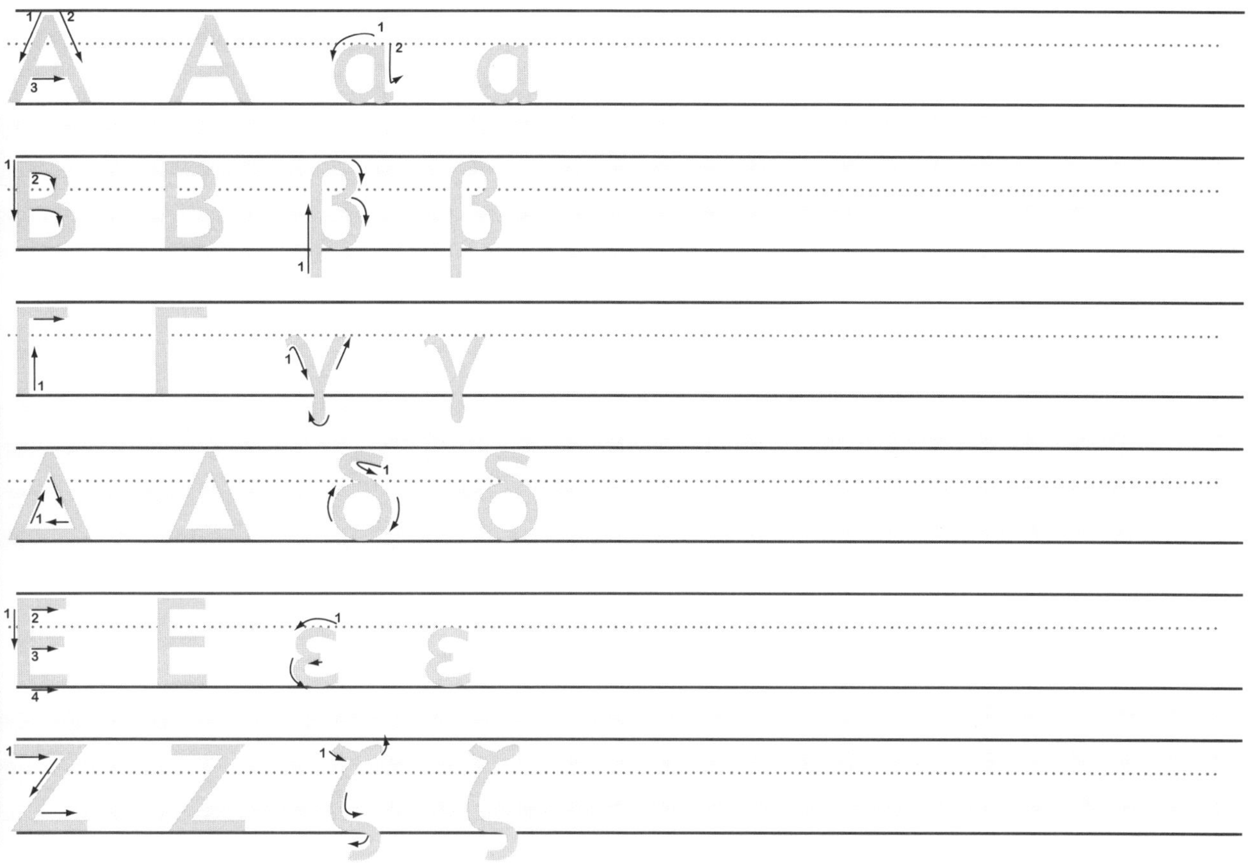

Α Α α α

Β Β β β

Γ Γ γ γ

Δ Δ δ δ

Ε Ε ε ε

Ζ Ζ ζ ζ

Now let's build some code words! Just as in English, we can put Greek letters together to form words. For example, we can put the English letters **b**, **e**, and **d** together to form the word **bed**. What Greek letters would you use to make the same word? How about **β**, **ε**, and **δ**? In Greek that would be **βεδ**. The chart below shows some other words you can make using Greek letters.

Cyphers

English Letters	Greek Letters
bed	βεδ
bag	βαγ
beg	βεγ
bad	βαδ
zag	ζαγ
gag	γαγ

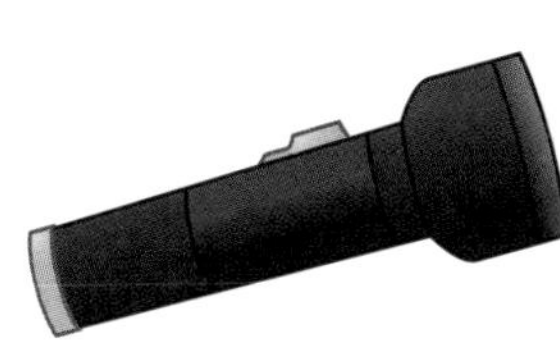

Now write each of these new words four times using Greek letters. Say each word as you write it. Pay attention to the uppercase Greek words at the bottom of the list—they're tricky!

Training Exercise

βεδ	________________
βαγ	________________
βεγ	________________
βαδ	________________
ζαγ	________________
γαγ	________________
ΒΕΔ	________________
ΒΑΓ	________________
ΒΕΓ	________________
ΒΑΔ	________________
ΖΑΓ	________________
ΓΑΓ	________________

Using your code-cracking skills from this chapter, can you decode this message?

Don't γ–α–γ on a β–α–δ ε–γ–γ!

Fill in the English:

Don't _____-_____-_____ on a

_____-_____-_____ _____-_____-_____!

Circle the word spelled in Greek letters that matches the English word at the beginning of the row:

Training Exercise

bed	βεδ	βαδ	δεβ	βεβ
gag	γεγ	γαδ	δαγ	γαγ
deb	βεδ	δεβ	δεγ	δαβ
bad	δαβ	δαδ	βεδ	βαδ
beg	βαγ	βεγ	γαβ	γεβ
dad	δαδ	δεδ	δαγ	γαδ
zag	ζαβ	ζεγ	ζαγ	γαζ
ebb	εγγ	εββ	αββ	εζζ
zazz	γαγγ	ζαζζ	ζαββ	ζεζζ
gab	γαβ	βαγ	βεγ	γεβ
egg	εζζ	εγγ	εββ	εδδ

Robbery Witness #4: Security Guard

"I could have been in the Secret Service, you know, but I figured it's more important to protect these priceless pieces of history that have been around for centuries, even decades. So, anyway, when I heard the αλαρμ I ran to the βακ door, ya know, to apprehend the perpetrator. I know how the criminal mind works, and I figured he would probably use that exit, unless he wanted his hand stamped for re-entry. When I got there, I was too late to catch the thief, but I found this βυτ print."

English Words:

#1: ___ ___ ___ ___ ___

#2: ___ ___ ___ ___

#3: ___ ___ ___ ___

Now spell the following English words using Greek letters:

Cypher Drill

English	Greek
bed	βεδ
bag	______________
beg	______________
bad	______________
zag	______________
gag	______________

To keep your skills sharp, complete the following word search. The word list uses Greek letters, but you must find the matching words in English letters. Before starting the word search, you may want to translate the Greek-letter words into English. As you're doing the puzzle, be sure to look for words diagonally and backwards!

Code Puzzle

I	R	B	K	J	R	B	G	H	C	D	U
N	A	D	Z	B	I	E	W	G	A	G	M
D	A	G	A	G	E	D	A	D	A	Z	Y
B	H	I	I	M	C	Z	W	X	F	U	K
R	C	C	B	W	F	N	R	M	B	L	A
B	E	G	B	A	G	K	P	B	P	O	S

ΒΕΔ ____ ____ ____ **ΓΑΓ** ____ ____ ____

ΒΑΔ ____ ____ ____ **ΖΑΓ** ____ ____ ____

ΒΕΓ ____ ____ ____ **ΔΑΔ** ____ ____ ____

ΒΑΓ ____ ____ ____ **ΔΑΒ** ____ ____ ____

Escape Route Witness Reports

Congratulations, Detective! You have discovered the identity of the thief! Go to page 66 and write the thief's name in the space provided.

Your work is not done, however. After exiting the museum with the stolen urn, the thief drove all over town before finally hiding the treasure. Now that you have identified the thief, we need you to find where they put the urn.

Luckily, we have several witnesses who saw the thief driving around town. Please carefully look over the clues, which are provided in your new, handy-dandy Spi*Tek device. As before, use your code-cracking skills to change the red Greek letters to English letters.

For each clue, **use the information provided to trace the thief's trail on the map on page 18 by using a pen or marker to mark each direction the witnesses mention**. Once you have traced the entire path, you should know where the urn has been hidden and the entire crime will be solved! Make sure that you follow each of the directions in order or you may not get the correct answer. Please note that the first one is already marked on the map for you.

Good luck!

SPI*TEK
Escape Route Witness #1:
Garbage Collector
"Yeah, I was emptying the dumpster νιρ the museum when I saw someone carrying a large pot run from the βακ of the museum and jump into a χαρ. The person then sped out of the parking λοτ and headed west."

English Words:

#1: ___ ___ ___ ___

#2: ___ ___ ___ ___

#3: ___ ___ ___

#4: ___ ___ ___

HELP FIND THE STOLEN URN!

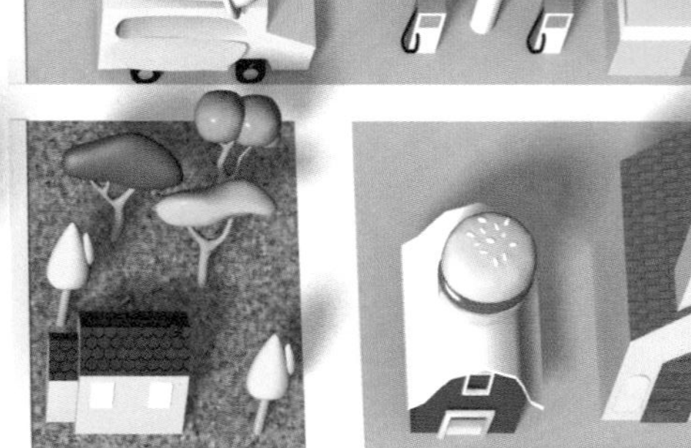

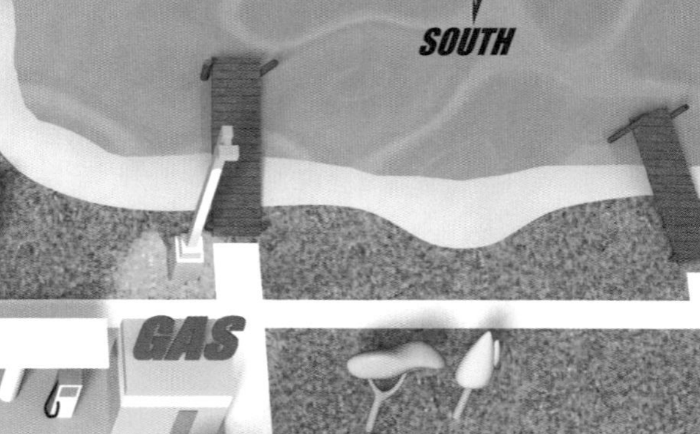

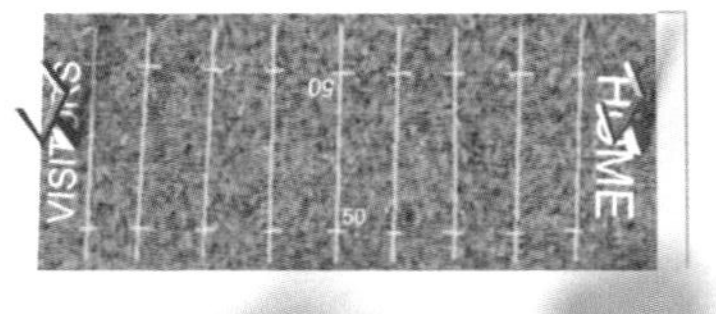
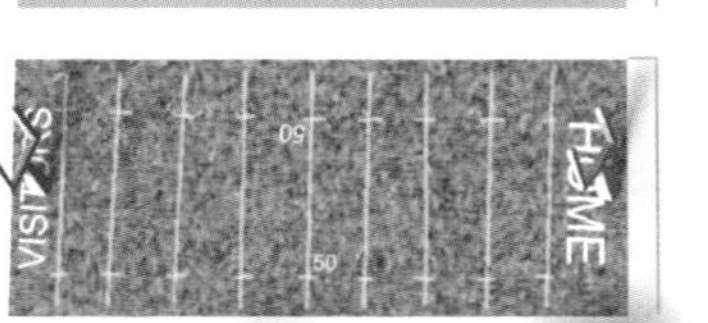

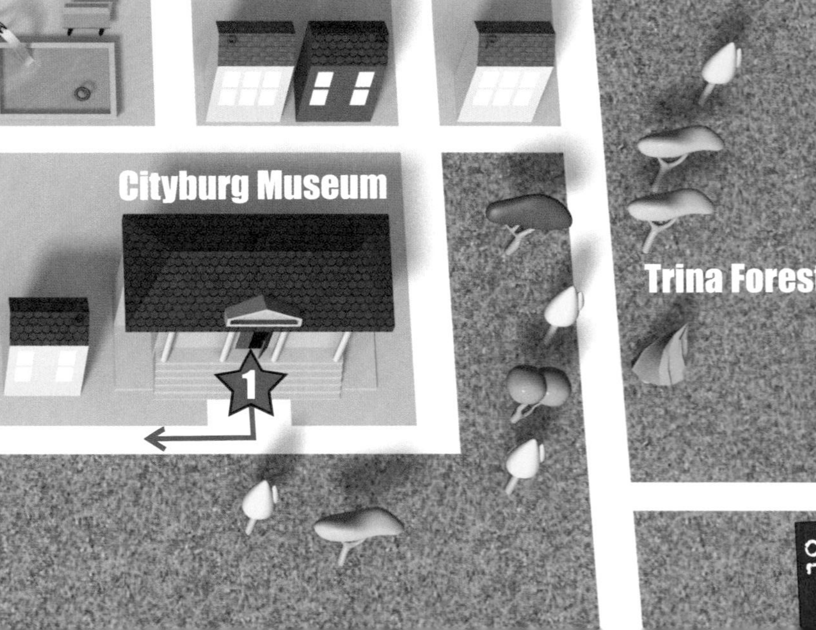

Mission Briefing:

The Next Six Letters

Now it's time to learn the next six letters in the Greek alphabet. The Greek letters ι, κ and μ look very similar to our letters that make the same sounds! Don't be fooled by the Greek letter **H**, though—it is an **eta** and makes a long **ay** sound, not the **huh** sound that our English **H** makes. For practice, sing through the Greek alphabet song and the Greek sound-off, making sure you can make the sounds for each of the six letters shown on the Cypher Card.

Draw a line to match each Greek letter with its name:

Eta	η
Theta	κ
Mu	ι
Kappa	θ
Lambda	μ
Iota	λ

Draw a line to match each Greek capital (uppercase) letter with its name:

Iota	Λ
Lambda	Η
Kappa	Θ
Mu	Ι
Theta	Μ
Eta	Κ

Circle the English letter(s) that make(s) the same sound as the Greek letter at the beginning of each row:

Training Exercise

Greek				
η	n	h	a as in ay	a as in ah
θ	q	th	t	o
ι	a	l	i	t
κ	c	k	r	h
λ	l	y	g	t
μ	n	w	u	m
Η	H	A as in ay	T	R
Θ	TH	O	H	E
Ι	L	T	I	Y
Κ	C	K	R	T
Λ	L	V	W	N
Μ	W	U	N	M

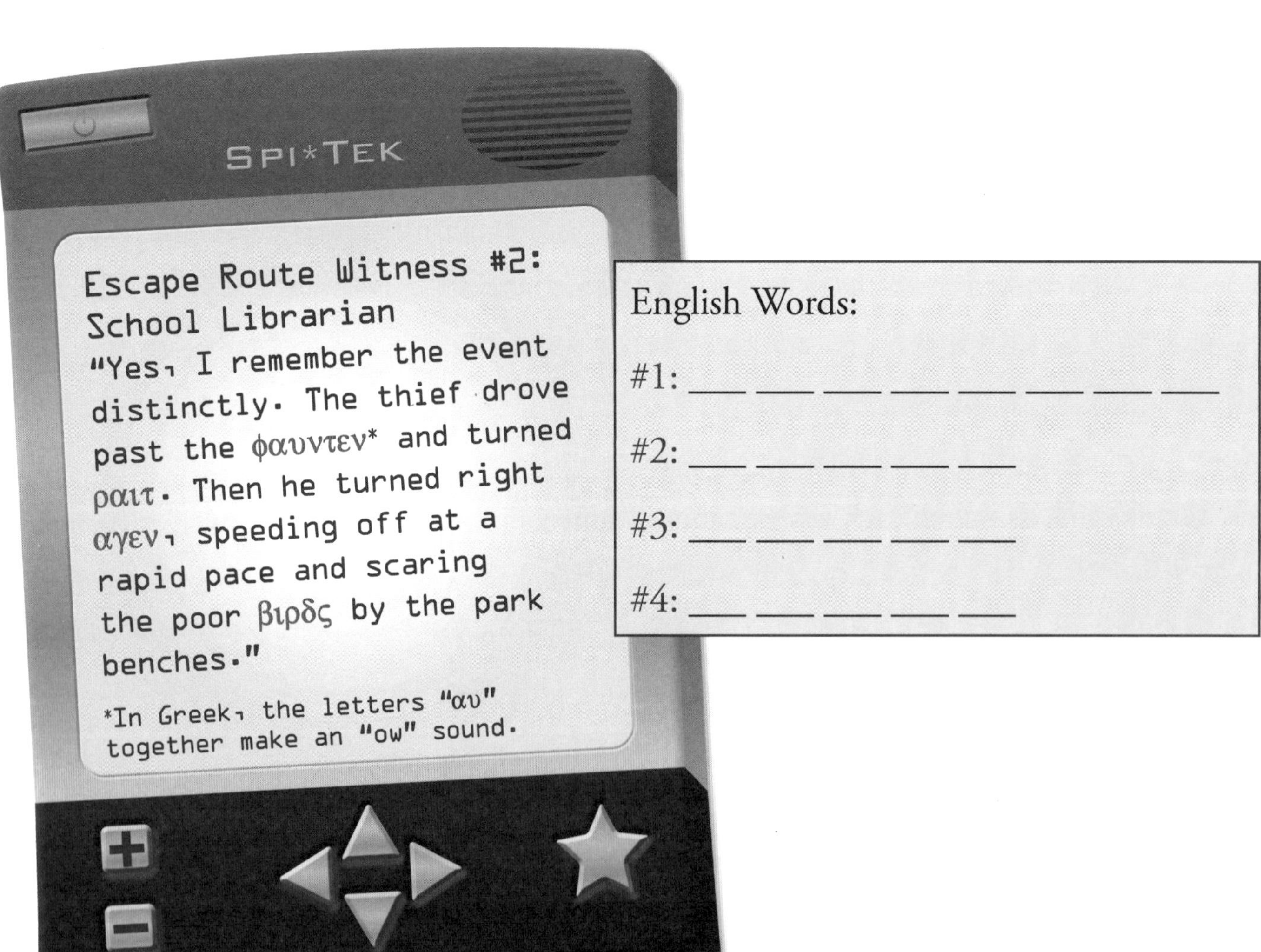
SPI*TEK
Escape Route Witness #2: School Librarian
"Yes, I remember the event distinctly. The thief drove past the φαυντεν* and turned ραιτ. Then he turned right αγεν, speeding off at a rapid pace and scaring the poor βιρδς by the park benches."
*In Greek, the letters "αυ" together make an "ow" sound.

English Words:

#1: ___ ___ ___ ___ ___ ___ ___ ___

#2: ___ ___ ___ ___ ___

#3: ___ ___ ___ ___ ___

#4: ___ ___ ___ ___ ___

Now let's practice writing all twelve of the Greek letters you have learned. As you write each letter, be sure to say out loud the sound it makes. Before you start, recite the Greek alphabet sound-off.

Cypher Practice

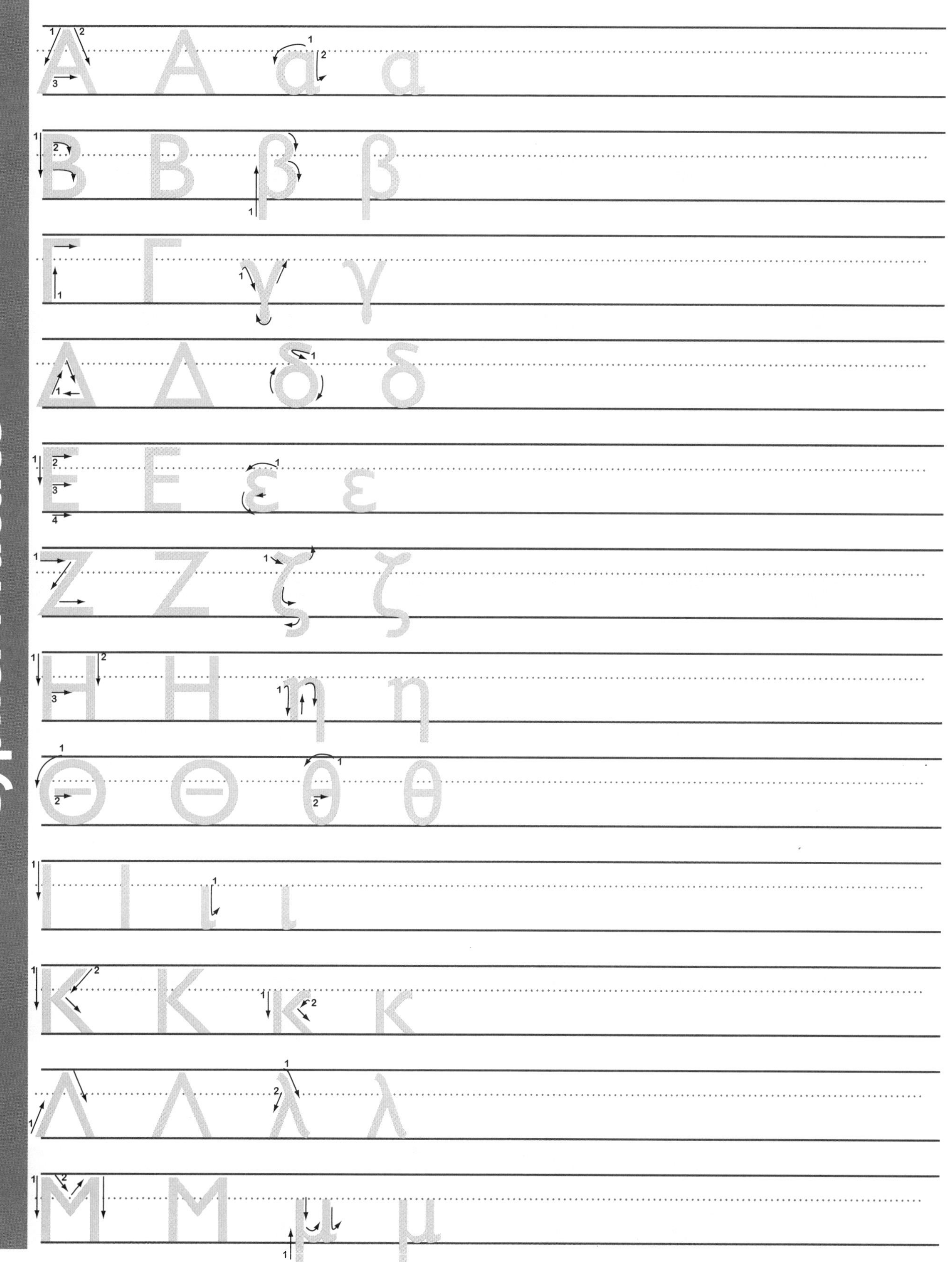

Now that you know twelve Greek letters, you can make more words than ever! First, though, let's practice making words with the letters you just learned: **η**, **θ**, **ι**, **κ**, **λ**, and **μ**. If we put the English letters **m**, **i**, **l**, and **l** together we can form the word **mill**. What Greek letters would you use to make the same word? You could use **μ**, **ι**, **λ**, and **λ**. In Greek that would be **μιλλ**. Look at the chart below to see some other words you can build with these Greek letters.

Cyphers

English Letters	Greek Letters
math	μαθ
kill	κιλλ
lake	ληκ
male	μηλ
lick	λικ
thick	θικ

Your Greek alphabet song and sound-off have taught you the sounds that each of these letters makes. The first two (**η** and **θ**) are the only ones that may seem strange. The last four (**ι**, **κ**, **λ**, and **μ**) look and sound like our English letters! Remember, though, that **η** makes an **ay** sound like our long English **a**, as in **rake**. Remember also that **θ** makes the **th** sound like the **th** in **thin**.

Look at the interesting words you can now make using the first twelve letters of the Greek alphabet!

Cyphers

English Letters	Greek Letters
mad	μαδ
lad	λαδ
bath	βαθ
leg	λεγ
keg	κεγ
bell	βελλ
Beth	Βεθ
lid	λιδ
kid	κιδ
dim	διμ
game	γημ
bake	βηκ

Now write each of these new words four times using Greek letters. Remember to say each word out loud after you write it.

Training Exercise

μιλλ	
ληκ	
λικ	
μαδ	
βαθ	
λεγ	
βελλ	
κιδ	
γημ	
βηκ	
ΜΙΛΛ	
ΛΗΚ	
ΜΑΔ	
ΒΑΘ	
ΛΕΓ	
ΒΕΛΛ	
ΚΙΔ	
ΓΗΜ	
ΒΗΚ	

Circle the word spelled in Greek letters that matches the English word at the beginning of the row:

Training Exercise

mad	μιδ	μαδ	μαγ	μαζ
bath	βεθ	βαβ	βαθ	θαβ
leg	γελ	ιεγ	λεγ	λαγ
bad	δαβ	δαδ	βεδ	βαδ
big	βαγ	βεγ	γιβ	βιγ
lag	λεγ	λαγ	γαλ	ιαγ
bake	βηκ	βακε	καβ	βικ
kid	κεδ	κιδ	κιγ	γιδ
zig	ζιβ	ζιζ	ζιγ	ζεγ
gab	γαβ	βαγ	βεγ	γεβ
Ellen	Ελλαν	Ελλεν	Ειιεν	Εγγεν

Now circle the English word that matches the Greek-letter word at the beginning of the row:

Training Exercise

μαδ	mid	mad	mag	maz
βαθ	beth	bab	bath	thab
λεγ	gel	ieg	leg	lag
βαδ	dab	dad	bed	bad
βιγ	bag	beg	gib	big
λαγ	leg	lag	gal	iag
βηκ	bak	bake	kab	bik
κιδ	ked	kid	kig	gid
ζιγ	zib	ziz	zig	zeg
γαβ	gab	bag	beg	geb
Εμμα	Enna	Ewwa	Euua	Emma

Now spell the following English words using Greek letters:

Cypher Drill

English	Greek
mad	μαδ
kid	______
beg	______
bath	______
thick	______
bell	______
zig	______
lame	______

Here's another puzzle to help you practice. Use the sounds of the words written in Greek letters to write the correct English words in the puzzle.

Code Puzzle

Across:

1. κεγ ___ ___ ___
3. λεδ ___ ___ ___
6. λαδ ___ ___ ___
7. λιδ ___ ___ ___
9. μιλλ ___ ___ ___ ___
10. μηκ ___ ___ ___ ___

Down:

1. κιδ ___ ___ ___
2. γαλ ___ ___ ___
3. λημ ___ ___ ___ ___
4. διμ ___ ___ ___
5. βελλ ___ ___ ___ ___
6. λεγ ___ ___ ___
8. δημ ___ ___ ___ ___

Two-Part Cypher

code	1	2	3	4	5	6	7	8	9	10	11	12
letter	α	β	γ	δ	ε	ζ	η	θ	ι	κ	λ	μ

Using the secret code above, change all the numbers in the message bubble below into the matching Greek letters. Next, sound out the Greek-letter combinations and write the final message using English words that match those sounds.

Help bring the 2-9-3 urn 2-1-10!
The 2-1-4 thief may 6-9-3 and 6-1-3,
but you can n-1-2 him.

Fill in the Greek letters:

#1: ______-______-______ #2: ______-______-______ #3: ______-______-______

#4: ______-______-______ #5: ______-______-______ #6: n-______-______

Fill in the English words:

Help bring the

______-______-______ urn ______-

______-______-______!

The ______-______-______ thief

may ______-______-______

and ______-______-______, but

you can **n**-______-______ him.

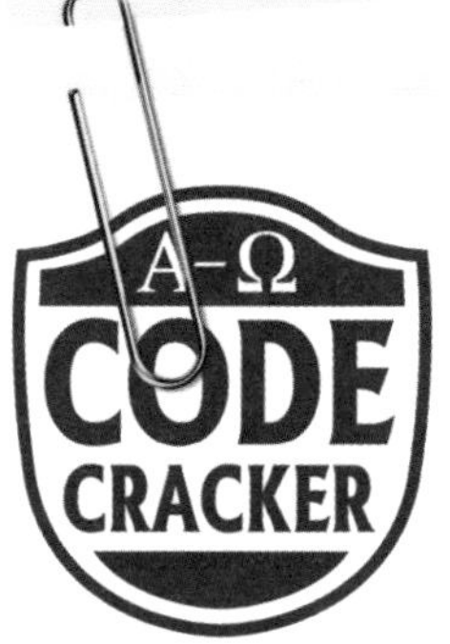

Mission Briefing:
The Next Six Letters

Now it is time to learn the next six letters in the Greek alphabet! Three of them look just like our English letters, but be careful—a couple of these letters are tricky! The Greek letter **Ο,ο** looks and sounds very much like our English letter **O,o**. The Greek letter **Ν** in the uppercase looks and sounds like our letter **N**. The lowercase version, **ν**, does not look like our **n**, however. Instead it looks like an English **v**.

The Greek letter **Ρ,ρ** looks just like our English **P,p** but makes the sound of our **R,r**! Instead, it is the Greek letter **Π,π** that makes our **P,p** sound! Think of freshly baked pie on top of the **Π** table and you won't forget the sound it makes.

Finally, there are two forms for the letter **sigma**: **σ** or **ς**. We use **ς** at the end of a word—so it is called a "final sigma." Everywhere else we use **σ**. For practice, sing through the Greek alphabet song and the Greek sound-off, making sure you can make the sounds for each of the six letters shown on the Cypher Card.

Draw a line to match each Greek letter with its name:

Rho	π
Xi	σ
Pi	ν
Omicron	ξ
Sigma	ρ
Nu	ο

Draw a line to match each Greek capital (uppercase) letter with its name:

Sigma	Ο
Nu	Ξ
Xi	Ν
Rho	Π
Omicron	Σ
Pi	Ρ

Circle the English letter(s) that make(s) the same sound as the Greek letter at the beginning of each row:

Training Exercise

ν	w	v	n	h
ξ	b	s	e	x
ο	u	o	a	c
π	p	r	h	w
ρ	p	r	g	d
σ	o	s	c	a
Ν	N	V	W	L
Ξ	TH	X	H	E
Ο	C	D	O	G
Π	P	R	M	W
Ρ	R	P	D	B
Σ	S	E	F	B

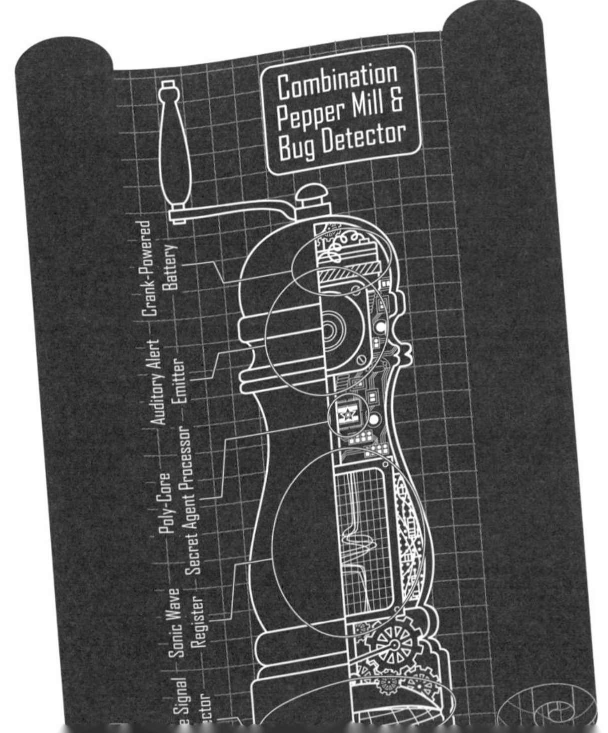

Now let's practice writing all eighteen of the Greek letters you know. As you write each letter, be sure to say out loud the sound it makes. Before you start, recite the Greek alphabet sound-off.

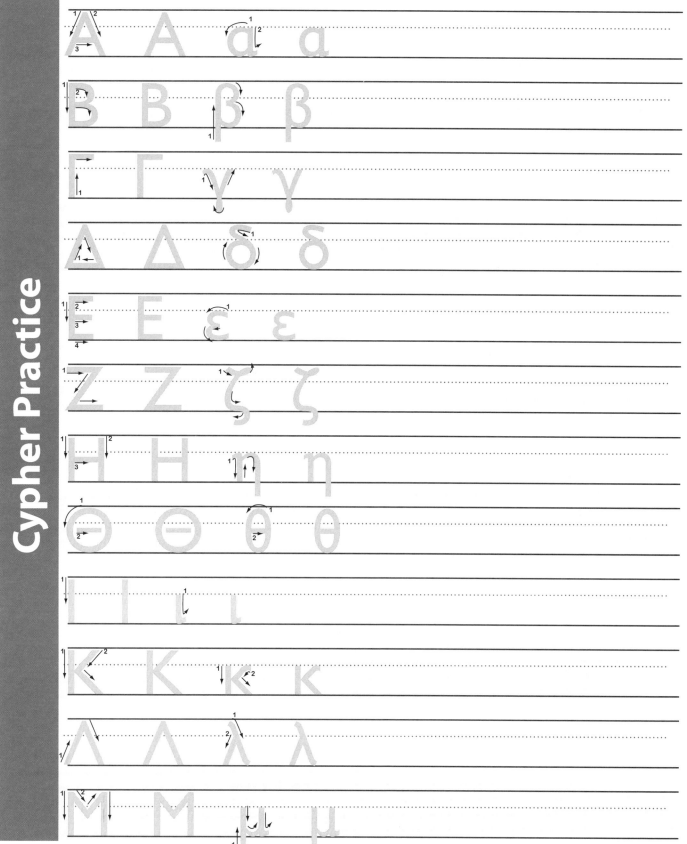

Cypher Practice

Α Α α α

Β Β β β

Γ Γ γ γ

Δ Δ δ δ

Ε Ε ε ε

Ζ Ζ ζ ζ

Η Η η η

Θ Θ θ θ

Ι Ι ι ι

Κ Κ κ κ

Λ Λ λ λ

Μ Μ μ μ

Now that you know eighteen Greek letters, you can make even more words! First, though, let's practice making words with the letters you just learned: ν, ξ, ο, π, ρ, and σ,ς. If we put the English letters **s**, **o**, and **x** together we can form the word **sox**. What Greek letters would you use to make the same word? You could use σ, ο, and ξ. In Greek that would be **σοξ**. Look at the chart below to see some other words you can build with these Greek letters.

Cyphers

English Letters	Greek Letters
sox	σοξ
pox	ποξ
sop	σοπ
Ron	Ρον
nor	νορ

Your Greek alphabet song and sound-off have taught you the sounds that each of these letters makes. Be careful with ρ—it is a **rho** and makes an **r** sound! Be careful also with ν—it is a **nu** and makes an **n** sound! And remember that at the end of a word the sigma looks like this: ς.

Now that you know eighteen Greek letters you can make many interesting words, like the ones below.

Cyphers

English Letters	Greek Letters
robber	ροββερ
car	καρ
man	μαν
path	παθ
ran	ραν
pan	παν
glass	γλαςς
map	μαπ
den	δεν
dentist	δεντιστ
bank	βανκ
zipper	ζιππερ
cane	κην
box	βοξ
boxer	βοξερ

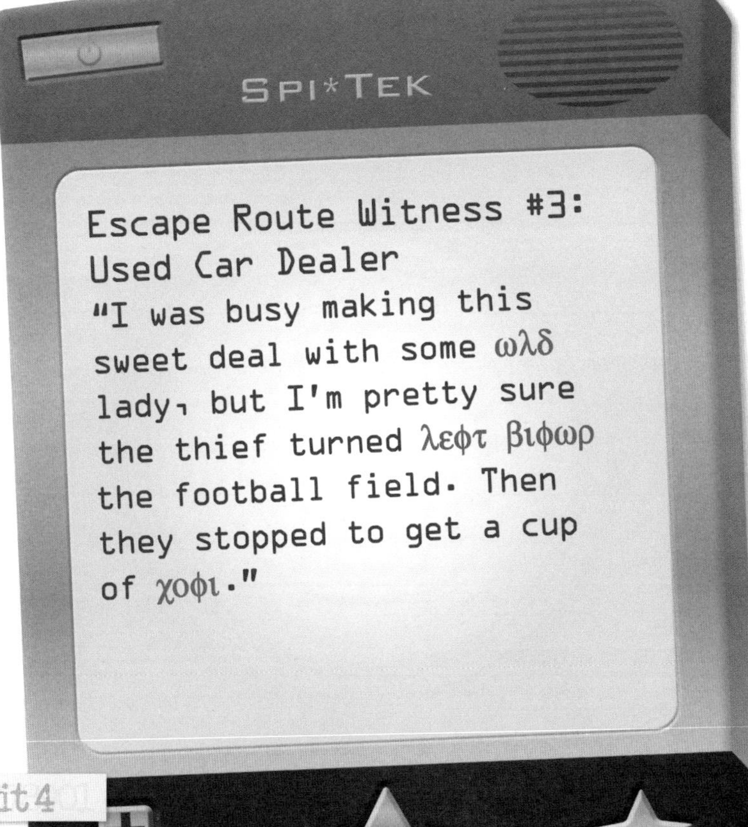

SPI*TEK
Escape Route Witness #3:
Used Car Dealer
"I was busy making this sweet deal with some ωλδ lady, but I'm pretty sure the thief turned λεφτ βιφωρ the football field. Then they stopped to get a cup of χοφι."

English Words:

#1: ___ ___ ___

#2: ___ ___ ___ ___

#3: ___ ___ ___ ___ ___ ___

#4: ___ ___ ___ ___ ___ ___

Now practice building some of these new words by writing them four times each using Greek letters. Remember to say each word out loud after you write it.

Training Exercise	
ροββερ	
καρ	
μαν	
παθ	
ραν	
παν	
γλαςς	
μαπ	
δεν	
δεντιστ	
βανκ	
ζιππερ	
κην	
βοξ	
βοξερ	
ΒΟΞΕΡ	
ΡΟΒΒΕΡ	
ΓΛΑΣΣ	
ΔΕΝΤΙΣΤ	

Circle the word spelled in Greek letters that matches the English word at the beginning of the row:

Training Exercise

robber	ροδδερ	ροββερ	ραββερ	ροππερ
car	γαρ	καρ	κερ	καπ
man	μαν	μεν	ναμ	νεμ
path	πατ	ραθ	παθ	θαρ
glass	γλασσ	δλασσ	γλαςς	γλιςς
map	παμ	μερ	μαρ	μαπ
den	δεν	δαν	δεμ	γαν
bank	βενκ	γανκ	ρανκ	βανκ
zipper	ζιββερ	ζιππερ	ζιππαρ	ζιγγερ
bag	γαβ	βαγ	βεγ	γεβ
box	βοκ	βαξ	βοξ	γοξ

Now circle the English word that matches the Greek-letter word at the beginning of the row:

Training Exercise

ροββερ	rubber	rapper	robber	rotter
καρ	care	cure	kur	car
μαν	mav	man	men	nan
παθ	rat	pat	path	tad
γλαςς	gliss	glass	blass	bless
μαπ	mop	mar	map	pam
δεν	den	dev	dew	dem
βανκ	bang	bing	band	bank
ζιππερ	zibber	zipper	zigger	zegger
κην	can	kav	cane	cave
βοξ	bos	boe	box	boz

Now spell the following English words using Greek letters:

Cypher Drill

English	Greek
robber	ροββερ
car	____________________
man	____________________
path	____________________
glass	____________________
map	____________________
den	____________________
bank	____________________
zipper	____________________
cane	____________________
box	____________________

English Words:

#1: ___ ___ ___ ___ ___

#2: ___ ___ ___ ___

#3: ___ ___ ___ ___ ___

#4: ___ ___ ___ ___ ___ ___

#5: ___ ___ ___ ___

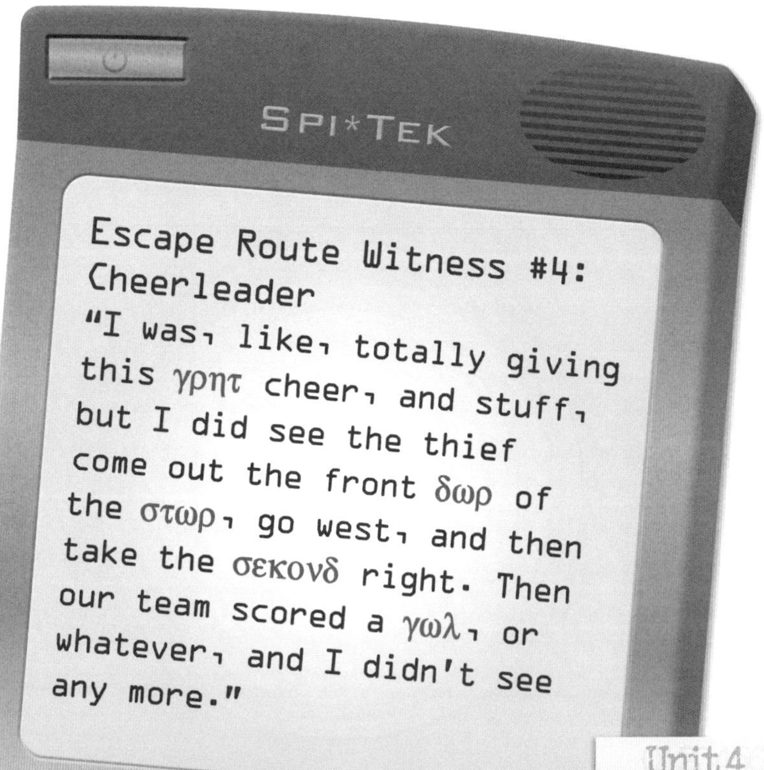

SPI*TEK
Escape Route Witness #4: Cheerleader
"I was, like, totally giving this γρητ cheer, and stuff, but I did see the thief come out the front δωρ of the στωρ, go west, and then take the σεκονδ right. Then our team scored a γωλ, or whatever, and I didn't see any more."

Two-Part Cypher

code	1	2	3	4	5	6	7	8	9	10	11	12	13	14	15	16	17	18
letter	α	β	γ	δ	ε	ζ	η	θ	ι	κ	λ	μ	ν	ξ	ο	π	ρ	σ,ς

Using the secret code above, change all the numbers in the message bubble below into the matching Greek letters. Next, sound out the Greek-letter combinations and write the final message using English words that match those sounds.

The thief says: "You may have 3-17-1-2-2-5-4 12-9, but you'll never 11-5-17-13 where I h-9-4 the 16-17-1-9-6."

Fill in the Greek letters:

#1: _____-_____-_____-_____-_____-_____-_____ #2: _____-_____

#3: _____-_____-_____-_____ #4: h-_____-_____

#5: _____-_____-_____-_____-_____

Fill in the English Words:

The thief says: "You may have

_____-_____-_____-_____-_____-_____-_____

_____-_____, but you'll never _____-

_____-_____-_____-_____ where I

h-_____-_____

the _____-_____-_____-_____-_____."

Here's another puzzle to help you practice. This time, use the provided English words to find the matching Greek-letter words. Be aware that some may be tricky because there may be more than one way to spell a matching word. Be sure to write out each of the English words in capital Greek letters before you try to solve the puzzle.

Code Puzzle

Β	Ρ	Ι	Κ	Υ	Μ	Θ	Ρ	Π	Τ	Λ	Υ
Α	Δ	Γ	Κ	Υ	Α	Α	Α	Χ	Ο	Β	Β
Ρ	Ω	Ν	Ε	Π	Ν	Λ	Ν	Π	Ν	Δ	Ρ
Δ	Α	Π	Ο	Π	Κ	Σ	Α	Ρ	Τ	Ε	Φ
Β	Ο	Ρ	Δ	Δ	Ε	Μ	Ν	Ν	Υ	Ν	Ν
Υ	Α	Λ	Ρ	Ρ	Ι	Π	Η	Ο	Τ	Ρ	Υ
Β	Ο	Ξ	Ε	Ρ	Α	Κ	Κ	Ν	Ρ	Ν	Η
Ν	Κ	Κ	Σ	Ν	Κ	Ν	Α	Φ	Ν	Π	Υ
Φ	Υ	Δ	Λ	Α	Υ	Λ	Ρ	Α	Α	Μ	Γ
Μ	Λ	Ξ	Ρ	Μ	Ε	Β	Π	Ν	Β	Ρ	Β
Τ	Ο	Ω	Χ	Ι	Ο	Τ	Β	Α	Τ	Ω	Ν
Β	Α	Π	Ω	Τ	Λ	Υ	Κ	Δ	Τ	Ε	Λ

CAR ____ ____ ____

MAN ____ ____ ____

PATH ____ ____ ____

RAN ____ ____ ____

PAN ____ ____ ____

MAP ____ ____ ____

DEN ____ ____ ____

BANK ____ ____ ____ ____

CANE ____ ____ ____

BOX ____ ____ ____

BOXER ____ ____ ____ ____ ____

NAP ____ ____ ____

RACK ____ ____ ____

COB ____ ____ ____

BRICK ____ ____ ____ ____

CLAP ____ ____ ____ ____

CAB ____ ____ ____

POP ____ ____ ____

UNIT 5

Mission Briefing:
The Last Six Letters

Now it's time to learn the last six letters of the Greek alphabet! Just like before, there are a few letters in this group that look and sound like our English letters and there are also a couple of tricky ones.

Let's look at the tricky ones first. The uppercase **upsilon**—Υ—may look like our English **Y**, but it sounds like our **u**, as in **glue**! Remember, there is no Greek **y**. The Greek letter **Χ,χ** looks just like our **X,x** but it really makes the sound of our English **k**, a hard **c** (as in **cat**), or a **ch** (as in **chorus**). The Greek letter **ω** looks like our **w** but it makes the sound of a long **o** (as in **bone**).

The Greek letter **Τ,τ** is an easy one, since it looks and sounds like our **T,t**. In contrast, the letters **Φ,ϕ**, **Ψ,ψ**, and **Ω,ω** are unlike any of our English letters, but they sure are strange and fun!

For practice, sing through the Greek alphabet song and the Greek alphabet sound-off, making sure you can make the sounds for each of the six letters shown on the Cypher Card.

Draw a line to match each Greek letter with its name:

Omega	ψ
Chi	ω
Phi	υ
Tau	χ
Psi	ϕ
Upsilon	τ

Now see if you can match the name of the letter to its corresponding capital (uppercase) Greek letter by drawing a line between them:

Upsilon	**Τ**
Psi	**Φ**
Tau	**Χ**
Phi	**Υ**
Chi	**Ω**
Omega	**Ψ**

Circle the English letter(s) that make(s) the same sound as the Greek letter at the beginning of each row:

Training Exercise

τ	t	f	l	i
υ	v	w	u	y
φ	o	d	p	f
χ	x	k	ch	y
ψ	p	ps	ds	ph
ω	o	w	u	m
Τ	L	T	I	K
Υ	W	Y	U	J
Φ	O	F	Q	G
Χ	K	X	CH	Z
Ψ	R	Y	B	PS
Ω	U	Q	O	W

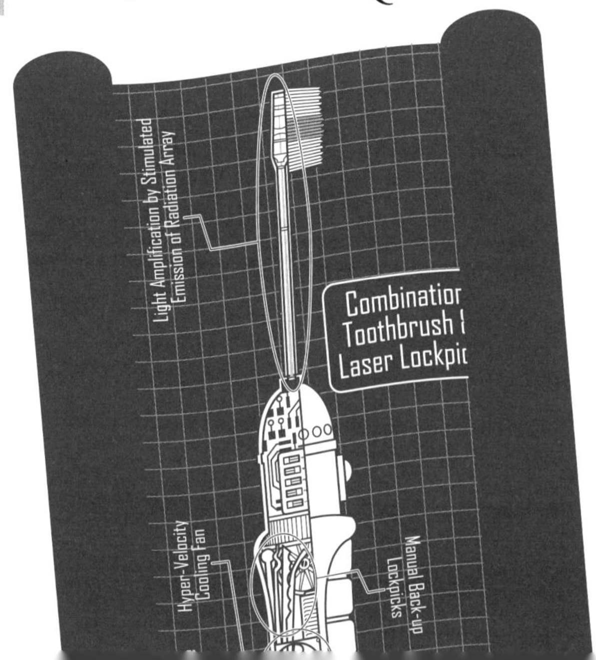

entire Greek alphabet—all twenty-four letters! As you
t loud the sound it makes. Before you start, recite the

Cypher Practice

α

Β β β β

Γ Γ γ γ

Δ Δ δ δ

Ε Ε ε ε

Ζ Ζ ζ ζ

Η Η η η

Θ Θ θ θ

Ι Ι ι ι

Κ Κ κ κ

Λ Λ λ λ

Μ Μ μ μ

Cypher Practice

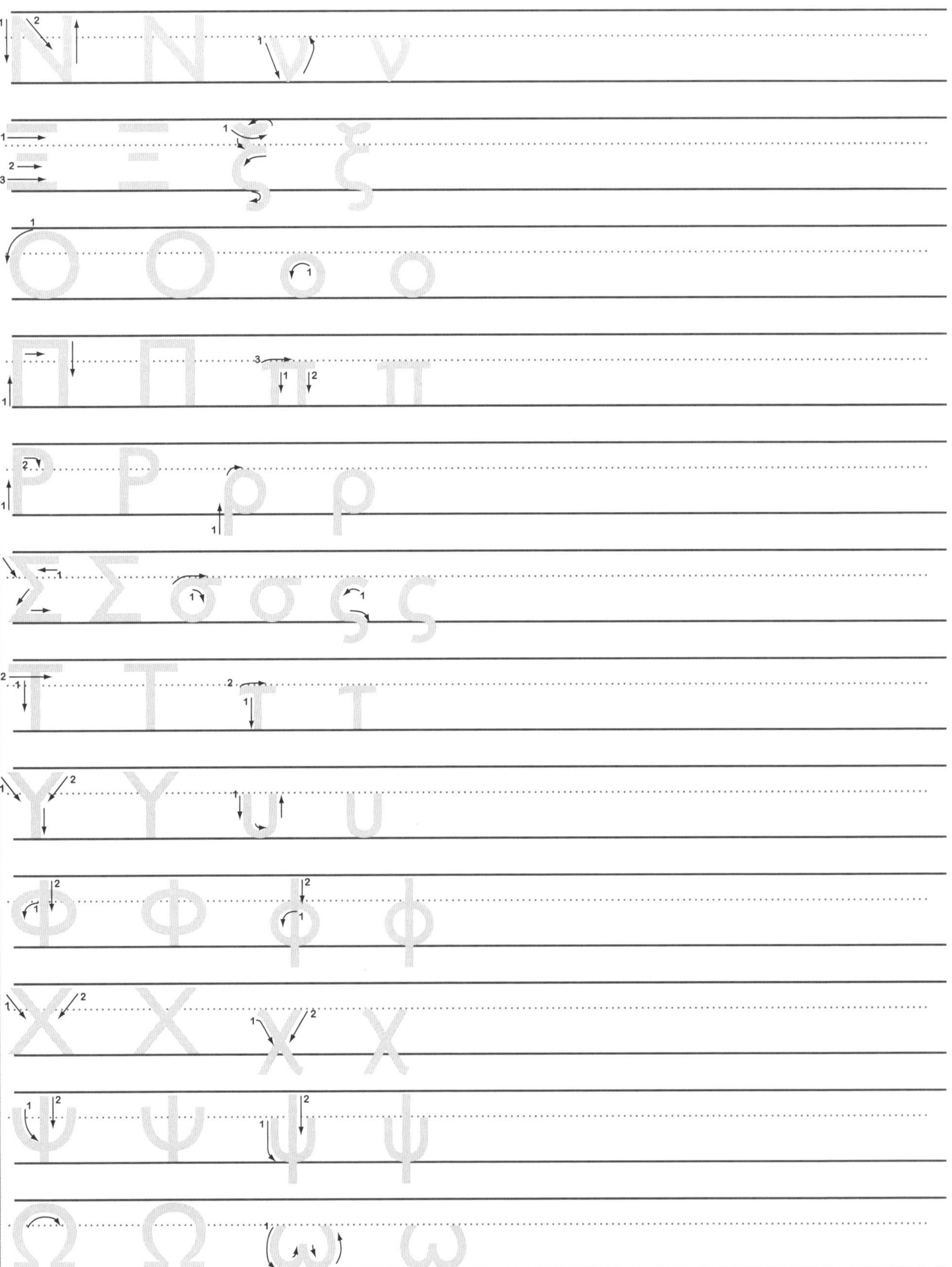

Now that you know all twenty-four Greek letters, you can make almost any word you want! First, though, let's practice making words with the letters you just learned: **τ**, **υ**, **φ**, **χ**, **ψ**, and **ω**. If we put the English letters **t**, **o**, **o**, and **t** together we can form the word **toot**. What Greek letters would you use to make the same word? You could use **τ**, **υ**, and **τ**, which would be **τυτ** (remember, a Greek **υ** is always a long **u** sound, as in **June**). The chart below shows some other words you can build with these Greek letters.

Cyphers

English Letters	Greek Letters
toot	τυτ
tote	τωτ
coat	χωτ
oops	υψ

Your Greek alphabet song and sound-off have taught you the sounds that each of these letters makes. Remember that **Υ** is an **upsilon** and makes a long **u** sound! Also, be careful with **ω**—it is an **omega** and makes a long **o** sound!

The following is just a very small sample of words you can make now that you know the entire Greek alphabet:

Cyphers

English Letters	Greek Letters
new	νυ
art	αρτ
clue	κλυ
bad	βαδ
gob	γοβ
broken	βρωκεν
in	ιν
road	ρωδ
street	στριτ
forbidden	φορβιδδεν
moon	μυν
all	αλλ
free	φρι

Now practice some of these new words by writing them four times each. Remember to say each word out loud after you write it.

Training Exercise

νυ	
αρτ	
κλυ	
βαδ	
γοβ	
βρωκεν	
ιν	
ρωδ	
στριτ	
φορβιδδεν	
μυν	
αλλ	
φρι	

Circle the word spelled in Greek letters that matches the English word at the beginning of the row:

Training Exercise

new	νεω	νυ	νοω	νω
art	απε	απτ	αρτ	ταρ
clue	κυλ	κλυ	κλω	κλε
bad	βιδ	δαβ	βαδ	βαρ
gob	γοδ	δογ	γααδ	γοβ
broken	βροκεν	βρωκερ	βρωκεν	βρωτεν
in	εν	ιμ	ιν	ον
road	ρωδ	ροδ	δορ	δωρ
street	στιτ	στριτ	στικτ	στεεπ
forbidden	φορβιττεν	φαρβιττεν	φορβικκεν	φορβιδδεν
moon	μυμ	μον	μυω	μυν
all	αιι	ακκ	αλλ	αττ
free	φριι	φρεε	φρυ	φρι

English Words:

#1: ___ ___ ___ ___ ___

#2: ___ ___ ___

#3: ___ ___ ___ ___

#4: ___ ___ ___ ___ ___

#5: ___ ___ ___ ___

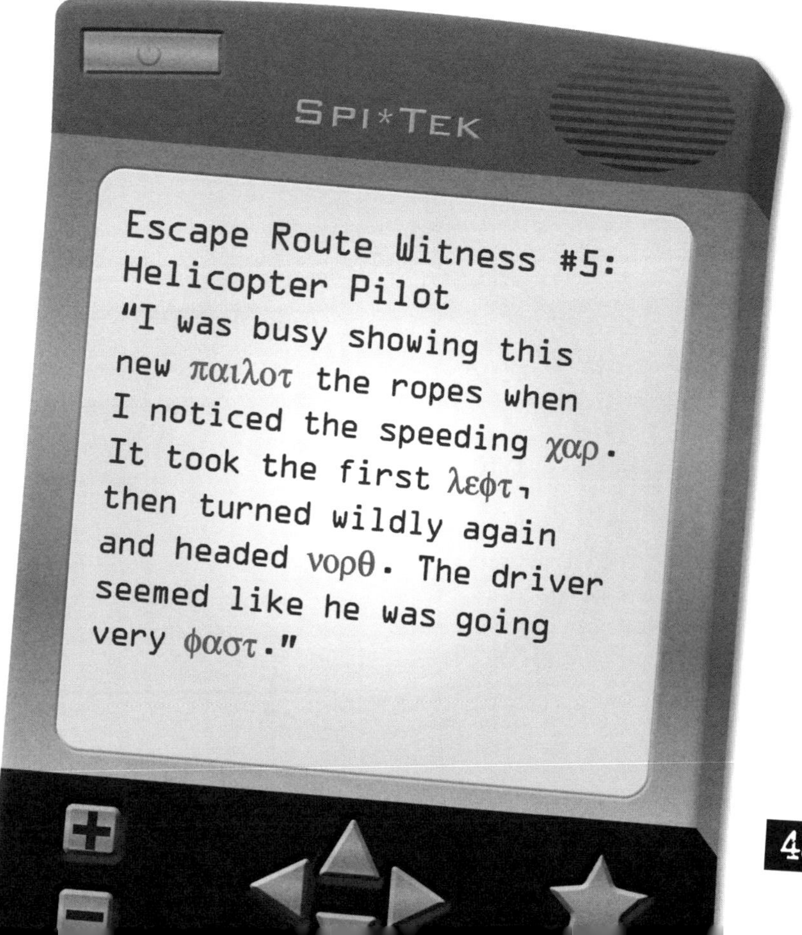
SPI*TEK
Escape Route Witness #5:
Helicopter Pilot
"I was busy showing this
new παιλοτ the ropes when
I noticed the speeding χαρ.
It took the first λεφτ,
then turned wildly again
and headed νορθ. The driver
seemed like he was going
very φαστ."

Now circle the English word that matches the Greek-letter word at the beginning of the row:

Training Exercise

Greek				
νυ	no	neo	new	knee
αρτ	urp	arm	ark	art
κλυ	glue	klu	clue	crew
βαδ	bid	bud	dad	bad
γοβ	gab	bug	gob	gut
βρωκεν	brick	brake	shaken	broken
ιν	on	it	in	un
ρωδ	ride	rope	road	read
στριτ	stick	strap	strict	street
φορβιδδεν	forbitten	forbidden	farbidden	forbikken
μυν	man	muck	mean	moon
αλλ	ill	al	all	at
φρι	fry	free	from	fro

Now spell the following English words using Greek letters:

Cypher Drill

English	Greek
new	νυ
art	______________________
clue	______________________
bad	______________________
gob	______________________
broken	______________________
in	______________________

Cypher Drill

English	Greek
road	______________________
street	______________________
forbidden	______________________
moon	______________________
all	______________________
free	______________________

Here's another puzzle to help you practice. This time use the provided English words to write the matching Greek-letter words.

Code Puzzle

Across:

1. all ____ ____ ____
3. potter ____ ____ ____ ____ ____ ____
5. boat ____ ____ ____
6. bad ____ ____ ____
7. bone ____ ____ ____
9. alone ____ ____ ____ ____

Down:

1. art ____ ____ ____
2. gob ____ ____ ____
3. pot ____ ____ ____
4. road ____ ____ ____
6. broken ____ ____ ____ ____ ____ ____
8. ran ____ ____ ____

1 2 3 4 5 6 7 8 9

Two-Part Cypher

code	1	2	3	4	5	6	7	8	9	10	11	12
letter	α	β	γ	δ	ε	ζ	η	θ	ι	κ	λ	μ
code	13	14	15	16	17	18	19	20	21	22	23	24
letter	ν	ξ	ο	π	ρ	σ,ς	τ	υ	φ	χ	ψ	ω

Using the secret code above, change all the numbers in the message bubble below into the matching Greek letters. Next, sound out the Greek-letter combinations and write the final message using English words that match those sounds.

You're doing 3-17-7-19.
Now that you know the 3-17-9-10
22-24-4, the thief doesn't
18-19-1-13-4 a chance.

Fill in the Greek letters:

#1: _____-_____-_____-_____ #2: _____-_____-_____-_____

#3: _____-_____-_____ #4: _____-_____-_____-_____-_____

Fill in the English words:

You're doing _____-_____-_____-_____-_____.

Now that you know the

_____-_____-_____-_____-_____

_____-_____-_____-_____, the thief doesn't

_____-_____-_____-_____-_____ a chance.

UNIT 6

Mission Briefing:
Consonant Blends

Now that you have learned all the letters of the Greek alphabet, you can form all kinds of words. Try writing some notes to others who know Greek—it's great practice! You can even create your own special code using what you've learned.

In this unit, you will learn about consonant blends, one of the last things you need to know about the Greek alphabet before you can start cracking the code of *real* Greek words! You'll learn the special sounds some consonants make when they are blended together, and then we will teach you some real Greek words. We will also teach you a special way to make the **h** sound.

What is a consonant? Consonants are "hard" letters that tend to close down the air that flows out of your mouth when you say them (like **t**, **s**, or **n**). Vowels are "soft" letters that make you open your mouth and let air keep coming out (like **a**, **e**, **i**, **o**, and **u**). The Greek vowels are α, ε, ι, ο, υ, and ω. All the other letters in the Greek alphabet are consonants.

Look at the chart below and try to make the sounds of all the blended consonants. You will probably be able to make most of the sounds because, in most cases, they make the same sounds as blended consonants in English. Check out those blends in the blue boxes, though. These are the tricky Greek blends because they are not like any of the letters we blend in English. The two consonants **πν** would be equal to our **pn**—which we don't see in English (unless a Greek word is being copied!). The same is true of **θν**, which would be equal to our **thn**—not a sound we make in English. Then there's **γγ**, which would be **ng** in English.

βλ	βρ	γλ	γρ	δρ	θν
θρ	κλ	κρ	πλ	πν	πρ
σλ	σρ	στ	στρ	τρ	φλ
φρ	νγ	γγ			

Since most of the consonant blends should be easy for you, let's study those easy ones first and then move on to the tricky ones. The following are the easy Greek consonant blends, which sound like English consonant blends:

Cyphers

Greek	English	Sound
βλ	bl	block
βρ	br	broom
γλ	gl	glad
γρ	gr	grape
δρ	dr	drop
θρ	thr	three
κλ	kl/cl	clock
κρ	kr/cr	cross
πλ	pl	plum
πρ	pr	prune
σλ	sl	sled
στ	st	star
στρ	str	strike
τρ	tr	trap
φλ	fl	flip
φρ	fr	frog

Now let's look at the Greek blends that are a bit tricky since they make sounds that we don't usually make in English. Listening to the online Tricky Greek Blend audio file (www.classicalacademicpress.com/greekcode) will help you to master these sounds.

Cyphers

Greek	English	Sound
νγ	ng	as in **ring**
γγ	ng	as in **ring**
γκ	nk	as in **drink**
γχ	nk	as in **drink**
θν	thn	sounds like "thunuh"
πν	pn	sounds like "puhnuh"

Circle the word spelled in Greek letters that matches the English word at the beginning of the row:

Training Exercise

English				
block	βλακ	βροκ	βλοκ	γλοκ
brat	βροτ	βραδ	βραπ	βρατ
glad	βλαδ	βλυδ	γλαδ	γρας
grass	γριvv	γραςς	γλαςς	γραππ
drop	δροπ	δριπ	δροv	δρυvκ
three	θρυ	θρεδ	θρι	θρε
clock	κλακ	κρακ	κλοξ	κλοκ
cross	κραςς	κριςς	κροςς	κλοςς
plan	πλαv	πλοτ	πλυμ	πλιμ
prune	πρυv	πρικ	πριμ	πρυμ
sled	σλετ	σλιπ	σλεδ	σλυμ
star	στιρ	στεπ	σταρ	στοπ
strip	στρυκ	στικ	στεπ	στριπ
trap	τρικ	τριπ	παρτ	τραπ
flip	φλοπ	φλικ	φλιπ	φιλιπ
frog	φραγ	φριγ	φρογ	γροφ

English Words:

#1: ___ ___ ___ ___

#2: ___ ___ ___ ___ ___ ___ ___

#3: ___ ___ ___

#4: ___ ___ ___ ___ ___

#5: ___ ___ ___ ___ ___

SPI*TEK

Escape Route Witness #6: Child on a Slide

"Yeah, sure, I saw the car. It went flying past the παρκ, then past the water tower. After that it looked like they στοππεδ for an αις κριμ. Then I couldn't see what they did because it was someone else's turn on the σλαιδ."

Now circle the English word that matches the Greek-letter word at the beginning of the row:

Training Exercise

βλοκ	black	block	blip	blot
βρατ	bret	brick	brat	brad
γλαδ	glad	glass	blood	glop
γρας	gram	grin	grass	grape
δροπ	drip	drum	drat	drop
θρι	the	three	threw	free
κλοκ	cluck	click	clock	clack
κρος	chris	crass	cron	cross
πλαν	plum	plan	plus	plot
πρυν	prune	prim	prick	prod
σλεδ	slot	slet	slip	sled
σταρ	store	star	stir	stap
στριπ	stick	step	strip	strep
τραπ	part	trap	track	trip
φλιπ	flick	flop	lips	flip
φρογ	frag	frog	frig	froy

English Words:

#1: ___ ___ ___ ___ ___

#2: ___ ___ ___ ___

#3: ___ ___ ___ ___ ___ ___

#4: ___ ___ ___ ___

#5: ___ ___ ___

SPI*TEK

Escape Route Witness #7: Gas Station Attendant

"I saw the thief drive right by our στωρ. He then turned and stopped at the dock by the λαμπ, renting a πaδδελ βωτ. You should have seen him working like crazy to move that thing, especially with that βιγ jar he had."

Let's see if you can match the Greek words on the left by drawing a line to the correct English words on the right. Be sure to pay attention to the consonant blends!

βλοκ	drop
βρατ	cross
γλαδ	plan
γραςς	strip
δροπ	clock
θρι	trap
κλοκ	frog
κροςς	glad
πλαν	block
πρυν	flip
σλεδ	three
σταρ	brat
στριπ	grass
τραπ	prune
φλιπ	star
φρογ	sled

You may be wondering about the sounds for **w**, **v**, and **j** in Greek. Sorry, but there are no Greek letters for those sounds! The best way to try and make a **w** or **v** sound is to use the Greek **φ**. The best way to make something like a **j** sound is to use the Greek **ι**.

What about the **h** sound? There is a way to make an **h** sound in Greek—at least at the beginning of a word. The chart below shows you two little breathing marks that come with the Greek alphabet. If a Greek word begins with a vowel, it will always come with either a smooth or rough breathing mark. The mark stands on top of the vowel unless it is a capital—then it is placed in front of the vowel. You will see the **smooth** breathing mark in front of a word that starts with a vowel (**α, ε, η, ι, ο, υ, ω**). The good news is that it is so "smooth" that it doesn't make any sound at all—it is silent. This mark looks like what we call an apostrophe in English.

Smooth	Rough
᾿	῾

The second breathing mark is the **rough** breathing mark. It looks like an English apostrophe that is facing in the wrong direction. You will often see this mark on top of (or in front of, if it's a capital) the first letter of a word that starts with a vowel (α, ε, η, ι, ο, υ, ω) or a ρ. A rough breathing mark tells you to make an **h** sound along with the letter next to it. Look at the examples below:

ἀτ	at	no sound
ἁτ	hat	**h** sound
ῥατ	rhino	**r** + **h** sound
ἰτ	it	no sound
ἱτ	hit	**h** sound

In the chart below, draw a line to match the Greek letters on the left to the correct English letters on the right. Pay special attention to the breathing marks! Remember, ᾿ makes no sound and ῾ makes an **h** sound!

ἑν	am
ἱπ	hot
ὀπ	helen
ἀμ	ot
ὡμ	en
ἑλεν	hen
ἁμ	hip
ὀτ	ellen
ἐλλεν	op
ἐν	ham
ὁτ	home

Your Name in Greek!

Do you think you can spell your own name in Greek now? Look at the samples below and then, using Greek letters, write your name in the space provided.

Susan	**Συσαν**
Ronald	**Ῥοναλδ**
Dan	**Δαν**
Jennifer	**Ιεννιφερ**
Linda	**Λινδα**
Matt	**Ματτ**

Your Name: ______________________________

Some *Real* Greek Words

Now that you know all your Greek letters, you can learn some real Greek words! Here is your first list of Greek words.

Cyphers

Greek	Pronunciation	English
ἀγάπη	ah-GAH-pay	love
καρδία	kar-DEE-ah	heart
κεφαλή	keh-fah-LAY	head
σοφία	so-FEE-ah	wisdom
φωνή	foh-NAY	voice/sound
χαρά	kah-RAH	joy
ψυχή	psoo-KAY	soul

Did you notice the smooth breathing mark on top of the first α in ἀγάπη? Remember, that mark is silent. But wait, what's that other mark doing there over the second α? Keep reading and you'll find out.

Accent Marks

The small accent over the second α in ἀγάπη tells you to give the accent to that syllable so that ἀγάπη sounds like ah-GAH-pay, with the accent, or emphasis, on the "GAH" syllable. In Greek you will see three kinds of accent marks: ´, `, and ˆ. Later in your study of Greek you will learn why there are three and not just one.

Practice your first real Greek words by writing each one three times in the space provided. Be sure to say the word out loud as you write it.

Training Exercise

ἀγάπη	______________________
καρδία	______________________
κεφαλή	______________________
σοφία	______________________
φωνή	______________________
χαρά	______________________
ψυχή	______________________

Here's another puzzle to help you practice your Greek alphabet. Use the clues listed to the right to unscramble each Greek-letter word and write the Greek letters in the correct blanks. Then write the letters marked with numbers in the matching numbered spaces below the puzzle to reveal a secret encoded message. In the space provided, write out the encoded message in English.

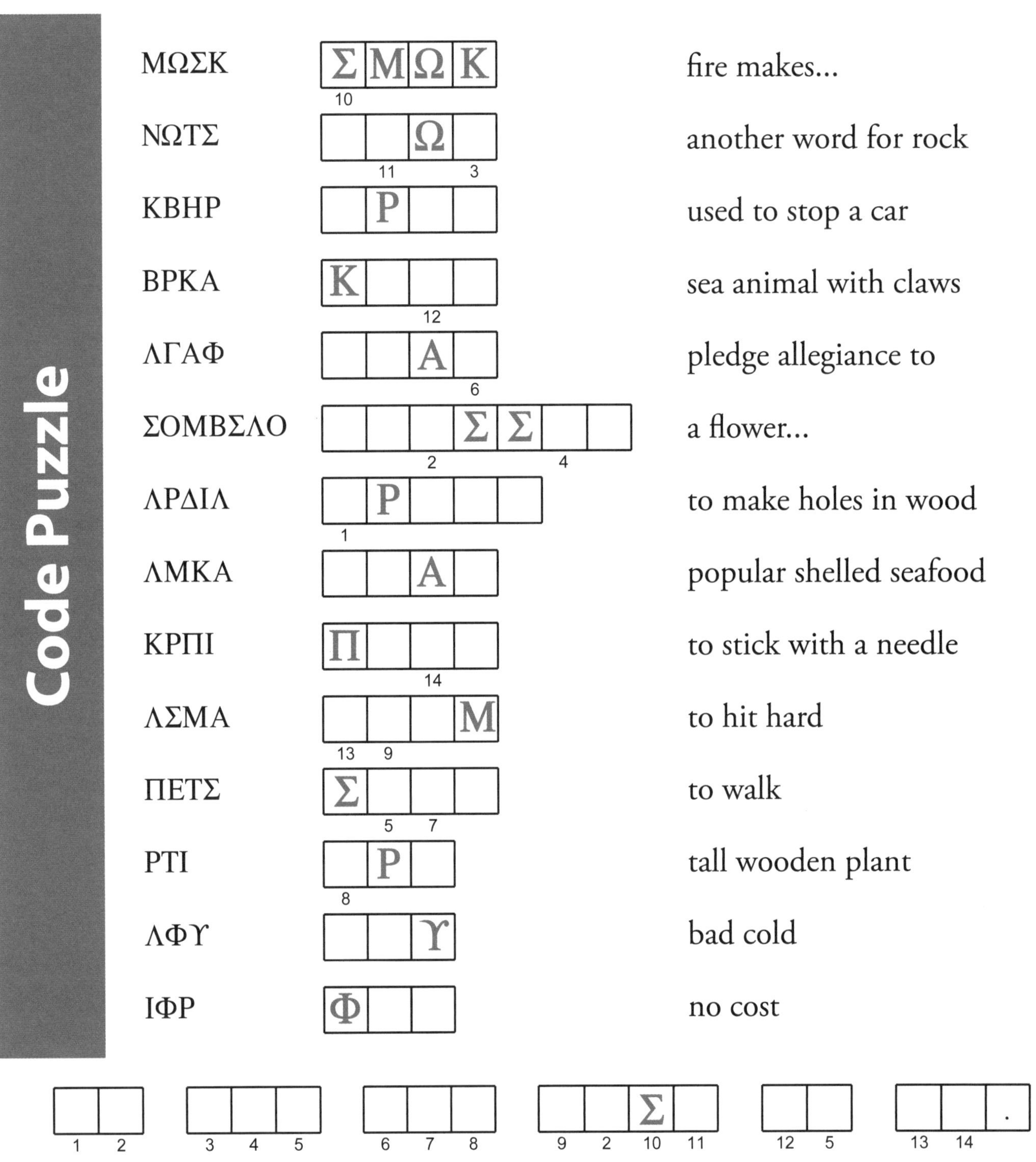

English: ____.

UNIT 7

Mission Briefing:

Vowels and Diphthongs

In the last unit you learned about consonant blends and how to make an **h** sound using a rough breathing mark. This week you will review the sounds vowels make and learn about some vowel blends—the special sounds made when two vowels are joined together. We call these vowel blends **diphthongs** (DIF-thongs). The word **diphthong** comes from a Greek word that means "two voices."

Here is a list of all the Greek vowels, along with their sounds:

Cyphers

Case		Name	Sound
Α	α	Alpha	ah
Ε	ε	Epsilon	eh
Η	η	Eta	ay
Ι	ι	Iota	ih or ee
Ο	ο	Omicron	aw
Υ	υ	Upsilon	oo
Ω	ω	Omega	oh

Did you notice that all of these vowels are "soft"? When you make the sounds for these letters, they make you open your mouth to let the air come out. Trying making the sound for **α**. Do you feel how the air keeps coming out of your mouth as long as you make the sound? Now try making the sound for **τ**. See how the air stops coming out of your mouth right after you make the sound? That is the difference between a vowel and a consonant.

Making Diphthongs

Did you know that we have diphthongs in English? Here are a few of them:

Cyphers	Diphthong		Sound	Example
	AI	ai	ay	bait/wait
	UE	ue	oo	Tuesday
	OA	oa	oh/owe	boat/float

Now let's look at a chart of Greek diphthongs. You can easily memorize the sounds these diphthongs make by listening to and learning The Diphthong Song available on the website (www.classicalacademicpress.com/greekcode)!

Cyphers	Diphthong		Sound	Example
	AI	αι	eye	aisle
	AΥ	αυ	ow	owl
	EI	ει	ay	make
	EΥ	ευ	yew	you
	OI	οι	oi	oil/boy
	OΥ	ου	oo	boot
	ΥI	υι	we	queen

The following are some examples of Greek-letter words that have these diphthongs:

βαικ	bike
αβαυτ	about
τεικ	take
φευ	few
βοιλ	boil
ρουμ	room
υι	wee
υιδ	weed

Now draw a line to match the Greek-letter word on the left with the correct English word on the right:

τεικ	weed
υιδ	about
ρουμ	take
υι	boil
βαικ	few
βοιλ	room
αβαυτ	wee
φευ	bike

English Words:

#1: ___ ___ ___ ___ ___ ___ ___

#2: ___ ___ ___ ___ ___

#3: ___ ___ ___ ___ ___

#4: ___ ___ ___ ___

#5: ___ ___ ___ ___ ___ ___

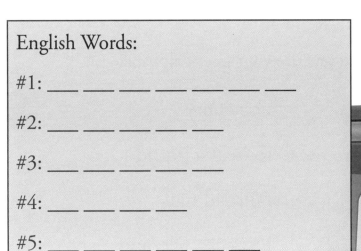

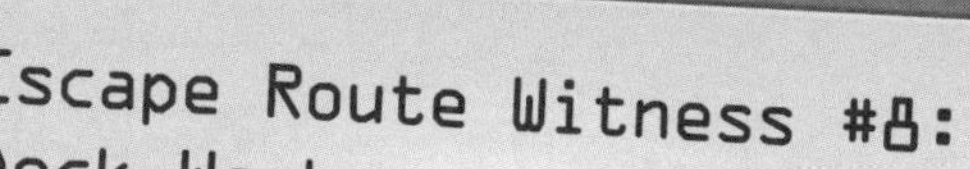
SPI*TEK
Escape Route Witness #8:
Dock Worker
"After several attempts at waterskiing, the thief gave up and docked at the pier by the βιγεστ beach--the one near the τρις. He hot-wired a πιζζα truck and headed βακ toward the σεντερ of town."

More *Real* Greek Words

Since you have learned all your letters, the smooth and rough breathing marks, consonant blends, and diphthongs, there is nothing keeping you from learning any new Greek word! The following is a list of several more Greek words.

Cyphers

Greek	Pronunciation	English
ἄνθρωπος	AN-thro-pos	man
κόσμος	KOS-mos	world
θεός	the-OS	God
κύριος	KOOR-i-os	lord/Lord
λόγος	LO-gos	word
παιδίον	peye-DEE-on	little child
τέκνον	TEK-non	child
υἱός	we-OS	son
βάλλω	BAL-loh	I throw
βλέπω	BLEH-poh	I see
ἀκούω	ah-KOO-oh	I hear

Here's another scramble puzzle to help you practice your Greek alphabet.

Code Puzzle

Scrambled	Boxes	Numbered box	Clue
ΦΥΕ	_ E _	5 (box 1)	not many
ΛΟΒΙ	B _ _ _	3 (box 2), 1 (box 4)	to heat a liquid
ΣΙΚΠΑ	_ _ _ _ K	6 (box 3)	railroad nail
ΒΥΙΤΕ	_ _ Υ _ _	8 (box 3)	Princess Sleeping ________
ΥΕΠ	_ E _	7 (box 1)	church seat
ΟΤΙ	T _ _	2 (box 2)	plaything
ΤΥΚΕ	_ E _ _	4 (box 1)	adorable

☐☐☐☐ (1 2 3 4) ☐☐☐ (5 2) ☐ (6) ☐☐☐☐☐. (7 2 8 1)

English: ____.

UNIT 8

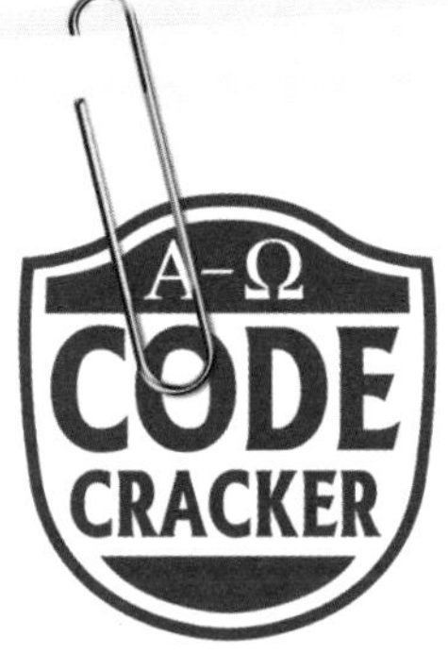

Mission Briefing:
Putting It All Together

Congratulations, Detective! You have learned everything you need to crack the code of the Greek language. From here you can go on to learn more and more Greek words so that you will be able to actually read Greek.

After all, reading a language is cracking the code of that language, isn't it? Each letter is like a little sign, or clue, and when those signs are put together in certain ways they make up words.

We get the word **code** from the Latin word **codex**, which means "tree trunk" and "wooden tablet." Some of the first books were made of thin wooden tablets tied together like pages. So, you could say that a code is like the writings in a book (a codex) that we read. A fancy word for reading is decoding, which means reading letters and words. Therefore, to read is to crack the code!

This week you will be reviewing the Greek alphabet just to be sure that you have it mastered. Let's begin.

The Alphabet

Try writing out the Greek alphabet from memory in the lowercase only. Then check your work by looking at the alphabet chart in the back of your book (page 68). The first and last letters of the alphabet are written in for you.

α

ω

Now try writing out the Greek alphabet in the uppercase (capitals).

Α

Ω

Greek to English

Translate the Greek-letter words in the first column into English words and write them in the second column:

Training Exercise

Greek	English
βουμ	
ρουφ	
απτελ παι	
ὁτ δογ	
ὡρν	
θιφ	
χλυ	
στρονγ μαν	

Translate the English words in the first column into Greek-letter words and write them in the second column:

Training Exercise	
stray cat	______________________
red flower	______________________
tall boy	______________________
cracker	______________________
dinner time	______________________
breakfast	______________________
black eye	______________________
milk and cookies	______________________

Consonants and Vowels

You have learned that the Greek alphabet has consonants and vowels. Remember that consonants are hard letters that cut off the flow of air out of your mouth when you say them. Vowels are soft letters that let the air keep flowing out of your mouth when you say them. You need both consonants and vowels to make words.

Circle all the vowels in the alphabet below, then write them out in the spaces provided.

α β γ δ ε ζ η θ ι κ λ μ ν ξ ο π ρ σ ς τ υ φ χ ψ ω

List of Seven Greek Vowels: _____ _____ _____ _____ _____ _____ _____

Blends and Diphthongs

Once you remove all six of the vowels from the Greek alphabet, you have eighteen letters left, and they are all consonants. There are several ways that you can blend consonants together to make "blended" sounds. The following are several Greek-letter words that have blends. Underline the blended Greek letters, then write out the English word and underline the blended English letters.

Cypher Drill

Greek	English	Greek	English
πρυν	prune	σλεδ	________
βραν	________	σταρ	________
γλοβ	________	στριπ	________
γριν	________	τρομβων	________
δροπ	________	φλιπ	________
θρι	________	φρογ	________
κλαπ	________	σλιμ	________
κρισπ	________	βλεςς	________
πλαν	________	κρυδ	________
βλυ	________	γλιττερ	________

SPI*TEK

Escape Route Witness #9:
Lifeguard at the Πουλ
"Dude, the truck drove past us, then turned λεφτ. Then I was like 'whoa!' because it took the first λεφτ and went παστ us on the οθερ side and then turned right."

English Words:

#1: __ __ __ __

#2: __ __ __ __

#3: __ __ __ __

#4: __ __ __ __

#5: __ __ __ __ __ __

Do you remember what a diphthong is? It is the blending of two vowels to make a new sound. Do you remember your diphthong song? If you do, you should have no problem filling out the box below:

Cypher Drill

Diphthong		Sound	Example
AI	αι	eye	aisle
AΥ	______	ow	owl
______	ει	ay	make
EΥ	______	yew	you
______	______	oi	oil/boy
OΥ	______	oo	boot
______	υι	we	queen

In the chart below, write the English word for each Greek word and then underline the Greek diphthongs that you find.

Cypher Drill

Greek	English	Greek	English
σκαι	sky	καιτ	______
αυλ	______	ταυν	______
τυδει	______	σνεικ	______
κευτ	______	βευτι	______
φοιλ	______	κοιν	______
τουτ	______	τρου	______
υικ	______	κυιν	______

Build Your Own Words

Why not build some words of your own? Simply take the letters from the Greek alphabet and make your own words, writing in the spaces provided! Be sure to provide the English translation of the Greek-letter words you write.

α β γ δ ε ζ η θ ι κ λ μ ν ξ ο π ρ σ ς τ υ φ χ ψ ω

Cypher Drill

Greek	English
______________________	______________________
______________________	______________________
______________________	______________________
______________________	______________________
______________________	______________________
______________________	______________________
______________________	______________________

English Words:

#1: ___ ___ ___ ___ ___

#2: ___ ___ ___ ___ ___ ___ ___

#3: ___ ___ ___ ___ ___ ___ ___

#4: ___ ___ ___

#5: ___ ___ ___ ___

#6: ___ ___ ___ ___ ___ ___

SPI*TEK

Escape Route Witness #10: New Βραιδ

"I remember that he pulled in next door while we were γεττινγ our picture taken under the στιπελ. We saw him park beside a nearby ρεδ building and walk around the βακ carrying a large vase and a tall λαδδερ."

Decode that Word!

The following is a list of real Greek words. Work carefully to decode these words and then say them out loud, being sure to pronounce them correctly. The first two are done for you.

Cypher Drill

Greek Word	English	Pronunciation
ἔχω	I have	EH-koh
λύω	I loose	LOO-oh
γράφω	I write	______________
διδάσκω	I teach	______________
λέγω	I say	______________
ἀγάπη	love	______________
κεφαλή	head	______________
φωνή	voice/sound	______________
ψυχή	soul	______________
ζωή	life	______________
γραφή	writing	______________

Simple Phrases

Here are a few simple Greek phrases (with pronunciation) that you will find useful. Be sure to practice them by reading them out loud.

Greek	English
Τί τὸ ὄνομα σού ἐστιν (TEE TAH AH-nah-MAH SOO es-teen)	What is the name of you? (What is your name?)
_____ ἐστὶν τὸ ὄνομά μου (_____ es-TEEN TAH AH-nah-MAH moo)	_____ is the name for me. (My name is _____.)
Ποῦ ἐστὶν _____ (POO es-TEEN _____)	Where is _____?

Use the clues listed to the right to unscramble each Greek-letter word and write the Greek letters in the correct blanks. Then write the letters marked with numbers in the matching numbered spaces below the puzzle to reveal a secret message. This message is the final clue in the Achilles Urn theft. Once you have decoded the secret message, write the thief's hiding spot in the space provided below.

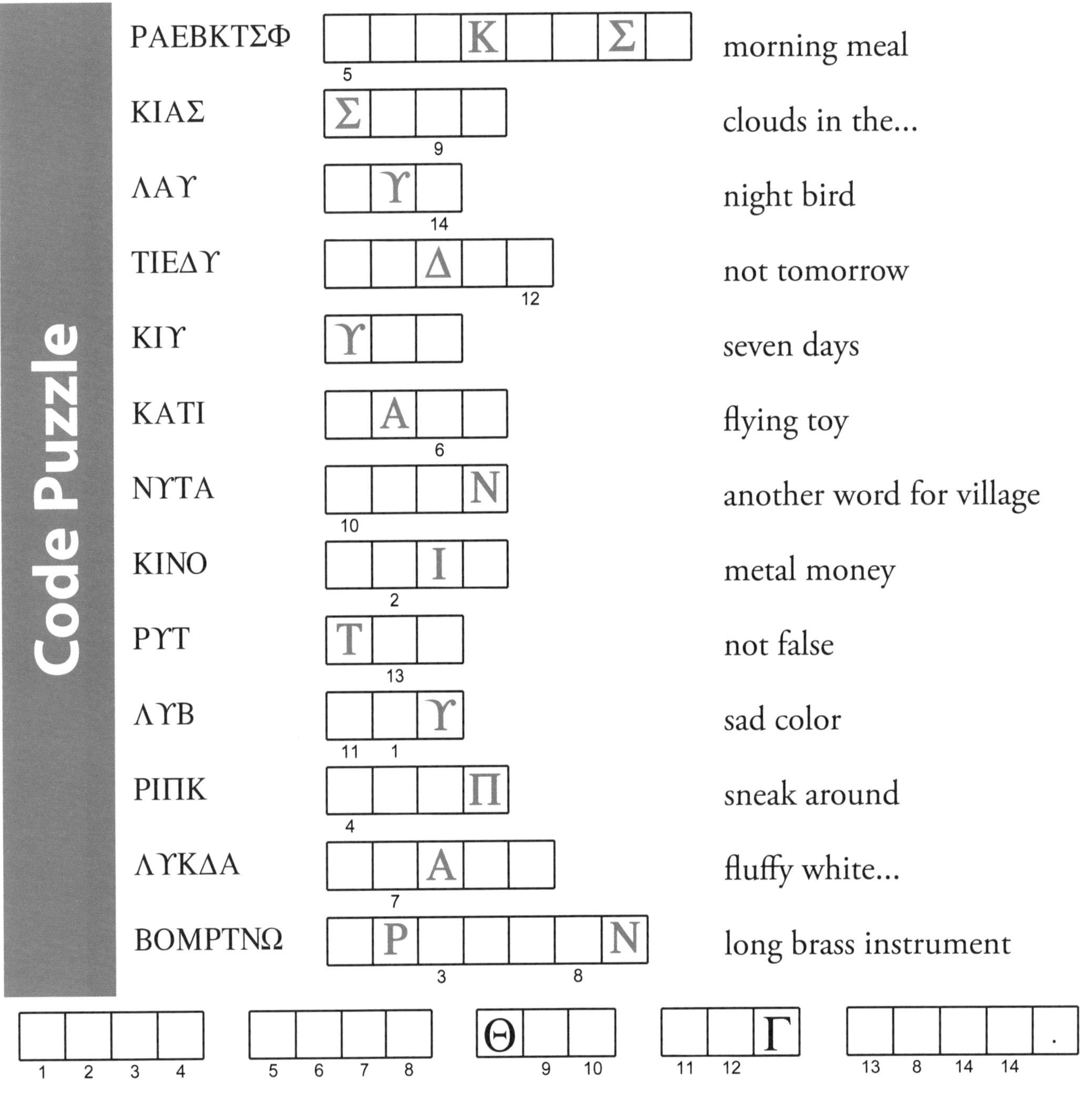

Code Puzzle
ΡΑΕΒΚΤΣΦ
K
Σ
5
morning meal
ΚΙΑΣ
Σ
9
clouds in the...
ΛΑΥ
Υ
14
night bird
ΤΙΕΔΥ
Δ
12
not tomorrow
ΚΙΥ
Υ
seven days
ΚΑΤΙ
A
6
flying toy
ΝΥΤΑ
N
10
another word for village
ΚΙΝΟ
I
2
metal money
ΡΥΤ
T
13
not false
ΛΥΒ
Υ
11 1
sad color
ΡΙΠΚ
Π
4
sneak around
ΛΥΚΔΑ
A
7
fluffy white...
ΒΟΜΡΤΝΩ
P
N
3 8
long brass instrument
1 2 3 4
5 6 7 8
Θ
9 10
Γ
11 12
.
13 8 14 14

English: ____.

Solution

The Thief's Name: ____

The Urn's Hiding Spot: ____

Mission Briefing:

The Greek Urn Caper

Congratulations, Detective! You have solved the crime and cracked the code of the Greek alphabet!

Since you have now mastered the Greek alphabet, you are ready to go on to *Song School Greek* (or another Greek book), in which you will easily learn over 100 new Greek words and many Greek phrases. Stay in touch, Detective, by visiting us at www.ClassicalAcademicPress.com, where you can play Greek Flash Dash to see how well you have learned your Greek words!

Don't forget to keep practicing your skills in order to always be ready. You never know when you'll be called on again to use your Code Cracker skills. Your skills are a privilege and a responsibility, so use them well.

Stay sharp!

Sincerely,

John Q Hoover

John Q. Hoover
Senior Code Cracker

Reference: The Greek Alphabet

Upper Case	Lower Case	Name	Sound
Α	α	Alpha	/a/ as in **father**
Β	β	Beta	/b/ as in **boy**
Γ	γ	Gamma	/g/ as in **got**
Δ	δ	Delta	/d/ as in **dog**
Ε	ε	Epsilon	/e/ as in **get**
Ζ	ζ	Zeta	/dz/ as in **cords**
Η	η	Eta	/ay/ as in **rake**
Θ	θ	Theta	/th/ as in **thistle**
Ι	ι	Iota	/i/ as in **pit**; /ee/ as in **ski**
Κ	κ	Kappa	/k/ as in **kite**
Λ	λ	Lambda	/l/ as in **lime**
Μ	μ	Mu	/m/ as in **math**
Ν	ν	Nu	/n/ as in **nose**
Ξ	ξ	Xi	/x/ as in **oxen**
Ο	ο	Omicron	/o/ or /aw/ as in **offer**
Π	π	Pi	/p/ as in **pistol**
Ρ	ρ	Rho	/r/ as in **rat**
Σ	σ,ς*	Sigma	/s/ as in **soup**
Τ	τ	Tau	/t/ as in **tea**
Υ	υ	Upsilon	/oo/ as in **hoop**
Φ	φ	Phi	/ph/ as in **phone**
Χ	χ	Chi	German /ch/ as in **Bach**
Ψ	ψ	Psi	/ps/ as in **oops**
Ω	ω	Omega	/ō/ as in **note**

*Sigma has two forms—σ and ς. The latter is called a final form and is only used when it is the final letter in a word. English used to have a similar custom using "f" for "s" when it was between letters.

Consonant Blends

Greek	English	Sound
βλ	bl	block
βρ	br	broom
γλ	gl	glad
γρ	gr	grape
δρ	dr	drop
θρ	thr	three
κλ	kl/cl	clock
κρ	kr/cr	cross
πλ	pl	plum
πρ	pr	prune
σλ	sl	sled
στ	st	star
στρ	str	strike
τρ	tr	trap
φλ	fl	flip
φρ	fr	frog
νγ	ng	as in **ring**
γγ	ng	as in **ring**
γκ	nk	as in **drink**
γχ	nk	as in **drink**
θν	thn	sounds like "thunuh"
πν	pn	sounds like "puhnuh"

Vowels

Case		Name	Sound
Α	α	Alpha	ah
Ε	ε	Epsilon	eh
Η	η	Eta	ay
Ι	ι	Iota	ih or ee
Ο	ο	Omicron	aw
Υ	υ	Upsilon	oo
Ω	ω	Omega	oh

Diphthongs

Diphthong		Sound	Example
AI	αι	eye	aisle
AΥ	αυ	ow	owl
EI	ει	ay	make
EΥ	ευ	yew	you
OI	οι	oi	oil/boy
OΥ	ου	oo	boot
ΥI	υι	we	queen

Chart of Breathing Marks

Smooth	Rough
᾿	῾

You will see the smooth breathing mark in front of a word that starts with a vowel (α, ε, η, ι, ο, υ, ω). It doesn't make any sound at all—it is silent. The rough breathing mark is often seen on top of the first letter of a word that starts with a vowel (α, ε, η, ι, ο, υ, ω) or a ρ. It tells you to make an **h** sound along with the letter next to it. Look at the examples below:

Breathing Mark Examples

ἀτ	at	no sound
ἁτ	hat	h sound
ῥατ	rhino	r + h sound
ἰτ	it	no sound
ἱτ	hit	h sound

Other Sounds

The best way to try and make a **w** and **v** sound is to use the Greek **ϕ**. The best way to make something like a **j** sound is to use Greek **ι**.

Accent Marks

In Greek you will see three kinds of accent marks: ´, `, and ˆ. These marks tell you on which syllable you are to put the emphasis. Later in your study of Greek you will learn why there are three and not just one.

Greek	Pronunciation	English
ἀγάπη	ah-GAH-pay	love
καρδία	kar-DEE-ah	heart
κεφαλή	keh-fah-LAY	head
σοφία	so-FEE-ah	wisdom
φωνή	foh-NAY	voice/sound
χαρά	kah-RAH	joy
ψυχή	psoo-KAY	soul
ἄνθροπος	AN-thro-pos	man
κόσμος	KOS-mos	world
θεός	the-OS	God
κύριος	KOOR-i-os	lord/Lord
λόγος	LO-gos	word
παιδίον	peye-DEE-on	little child
τέκνον	TEK-non	child
υἱός	we-OS	son
βάλλω	BAL-loh	I throw
βλέπω	BLEH-poh	I see
ἀκούω	ah-KOO-oh	I hear
ἔχω	EH-koh	I have
λύω	LOO-oh	I loose
γράφω	GRAH-foh	I write
διδάσκω	di-DAS-koh	I teach
λέγω	LEH-goh	I say
ζωή	zoh-AY	life
γραφή	grah-FAY	writing

Reference: Greek Alphabet Practice

Α α

Β β

Γ γ

Δ δ

Ε ε

Ζ ζ

Η η

Θ θ

Ι ι

Κ κ

Λ λ

Μ μ

Ν ν

Ξ ξ

Ο ο

Π π

Ρ ρ

Σ σ ς

Τ τ

Υ υ

Φ φ

Χ χ

Ψ ψ

Ω ω

Create Your Own Two-Part Cypher Message

Using your Greek skills, write out a secret message in the speech bubble below using the number code provided. To use the code, be sure to first sound out how an English word would be spelled using Greek letters, then write the numbers that match those letters. (Note: Keep in mind that some sounds are not possible in Greek, such as the **uh** sound in **the**.) After you write out your message, find another Greek Alphabet Code Cracker detective and see if he can read it.

code	1	2	3	4	5	6	7	8	9	10	11	12
letter	α	β	γ	δ	ε	ζ	η	θ	ι	κ	λ	μ
code	13	14	15	16	17	18	19	20	21	22	23	24
letter	ν	ξ	ο	π	ρ	σ,ς	τ	υ	φ	χ	ψ	ω

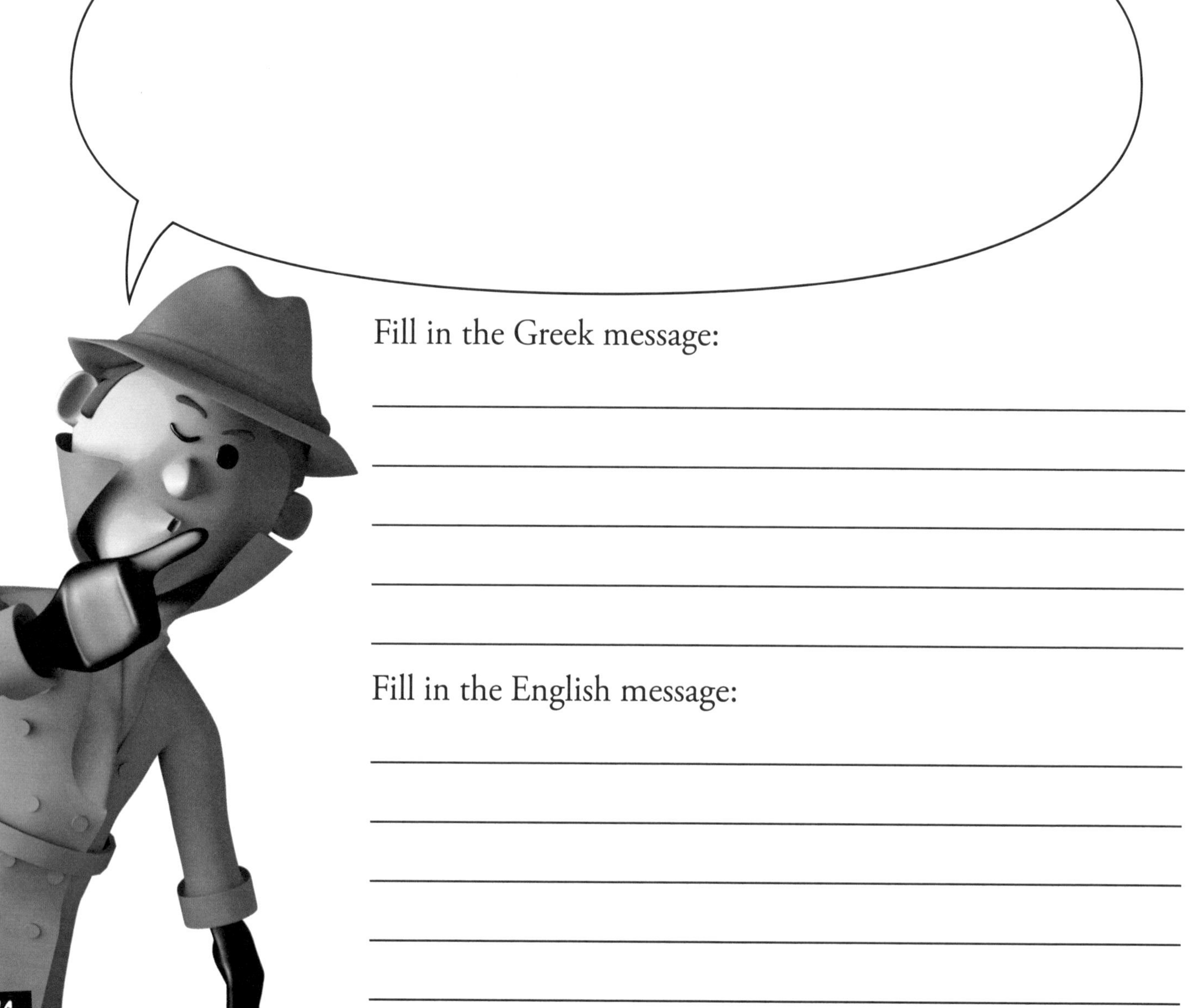

Fill in the Greek message:

____

____

____

____

____

Fill in the English message:

____

____

____

____

____

Create Your Own Two-Part Cypher Message

Using your Greek skills, write out a secret message in the speech bubble below using the number code provided. To use the code, be sure to first sound out how an English word would be spelled using Greek letters, then write the numbers that match those letters. (Note: Keep in mind that some sounds are not possible in Greek, such as the **uh** sound in **the**.) After you write out your message, find another Greek Alphabet Code Cracker detective and see if he can read it.

code	1	2	3	4	5	6	7	8	9	10	11	12
letter	α	β	γ	δ	ε	ζ	η	θ	ι	κ	λ	μ
code	13	14	15	16	17	18	19	20	21	22	23	24
letter	ν	ξ	ο	π	ρ	σ,ς	τ	υ	φ	χ	ψ	ω

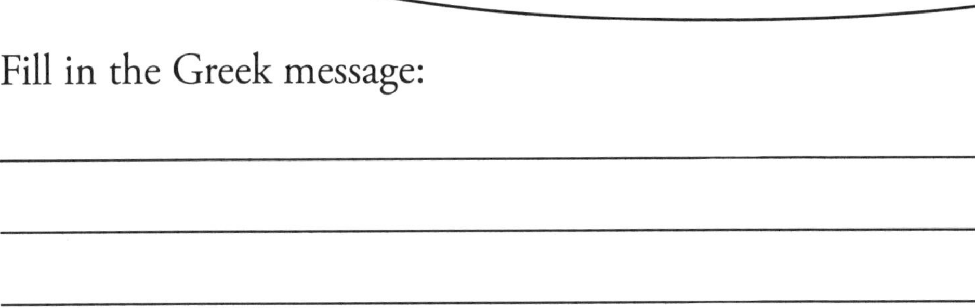

Fill in the Greek message:

____

____

____

____

____

Fill in the English message:

____

____

____

____

____

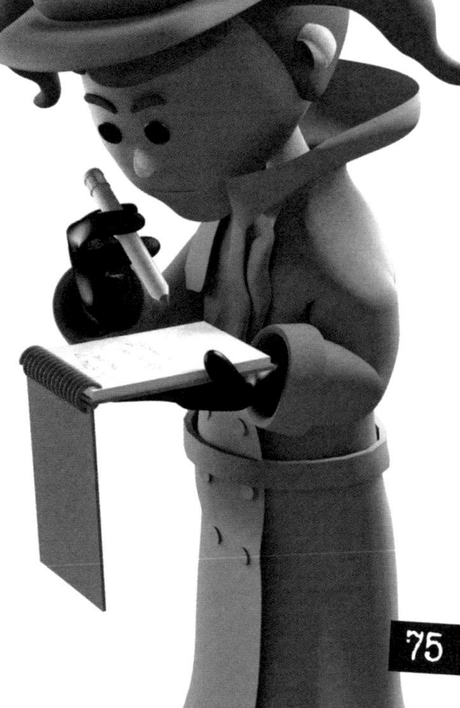

Greek Alphabet Code Cracker Cypher Wheel

1. Cut out the two pieces (this page and page 79) along the dotted lines.
2. (Optional) Glue the two pieces to cardboard circles cut to match.
3. Carefully cut out the small window in the cypher wheel top, indicated by the red X.
4. Using a brad, punch a small hole in the centers of both pieces (marked by the white crosshairs) and join the pieces, careful to keep the centers aligned (see Figure 1).
5. Spin the wheel on the axis created by the brad. When you point the arrow to a Greek letter, the matching English letter will be visible in the window.

Figure 1

Cypher Wheel Top

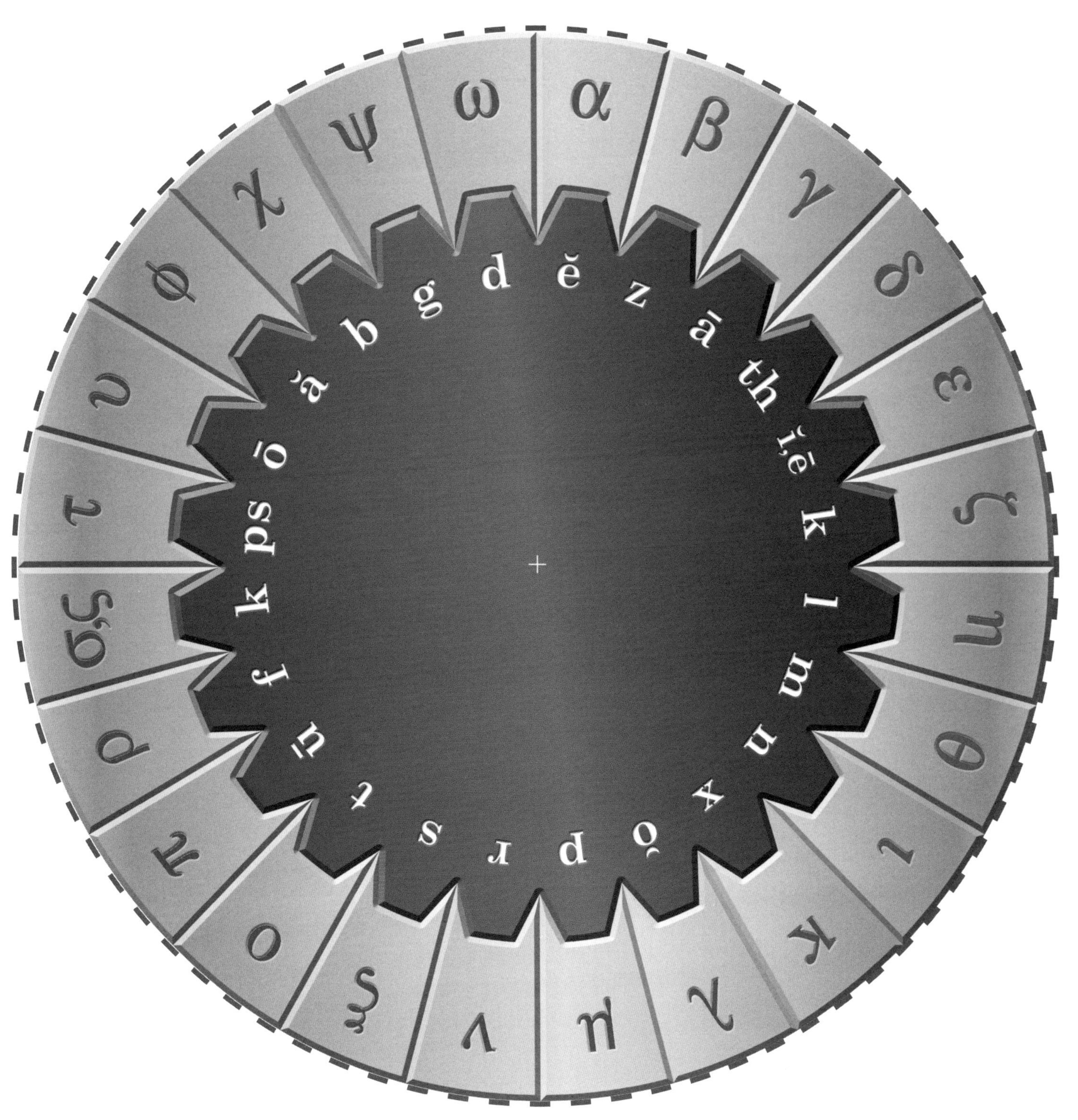

Cypher Wheel Bottom

Answer Key

Here are the English translations for all the Greek code words used in the witness reports scattered throughout the book.

Robbery
Witness #1, p. 8:
1. rare
2. fast
3. hat

Robbery
Witness #2, p. 10:
1. color
2. thief
3. glasses

Robbery
Witness #3, p. 12:
1. pot
2. time
3. timepiece

Robbery
Witness #4, p. 15:
1. alarm
2. back
3. boot

Escape Route
Witness #1, p. 17:
1. near
2. back
3. car
4. lot

Escape Route
Witness #4, p. 34:
1. great
2. door
3. store
4. second
5. goal

Escape Route
Witness #6, p. 49:
1. park
2. stopped
3. ice
4. cream
5. slide

Escape Route
Witness #9, p. 62:
1. Pool
2. left
3. left
4. past
5. other

Escape Route
Witness #2, p. 20:
1. fountain
2. right
3. again
4. birds

Escape Route
Witness #5, p. 43:
1. pilot
2. car
3. left
4. north
5. fast

Escape Route
Witness #7, p. 50:
1. store
2. lamp
3. paddle
4. boat
5. big

Escape Route
Witness #10, p. 64:
1. Bride
2. getting
3. steeple
4. red
5. back
6. ladder

Escape Route
Witness #3, p. 31:
1. old
2. left
3. before
4. coffee

Escape Route
Witness #8, p. 57:
1. biggest
2. trees
3. pizza
4. back
5. center

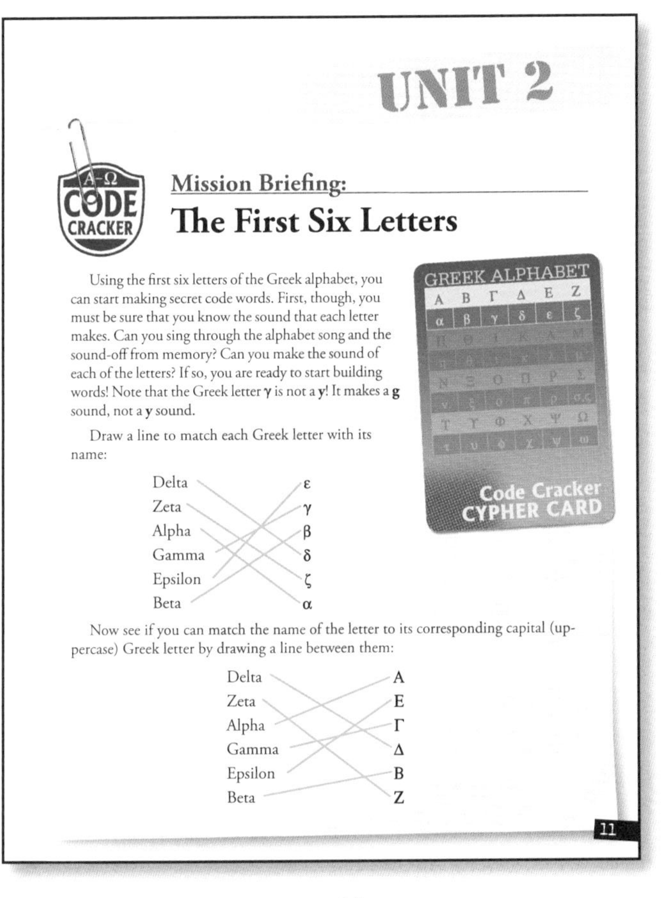

UNIT 2

Mission Briefing:
The First Six Letters

Using the first six letters of the Greek alphabet, you can start making secret code words. First, though, you must be sure that you know the sound that each letter makes. Can you sing through the alphabet song and the sound-off from memory? Can you make the sound of each of the letters? If so, you are ready to start building words! Note that the Greek letter **γ** is not a **y**! It makes a **g** sound, not a **y** sound.

Draw a line to match each Greek letter with its name:

Delta — δ
Zeta — ζ
Alpha — α
Gamma — γ
Epsilon — ε
Beta — β

Now see if you can match the name of the letter to its corresponding capital (uppercase) Greek letter by drawing a line between them:

Delta — Δ
Zeta — Z
Alpha — A
Gamma — Γ
Epsilon — E
Beta — B

11

page 11

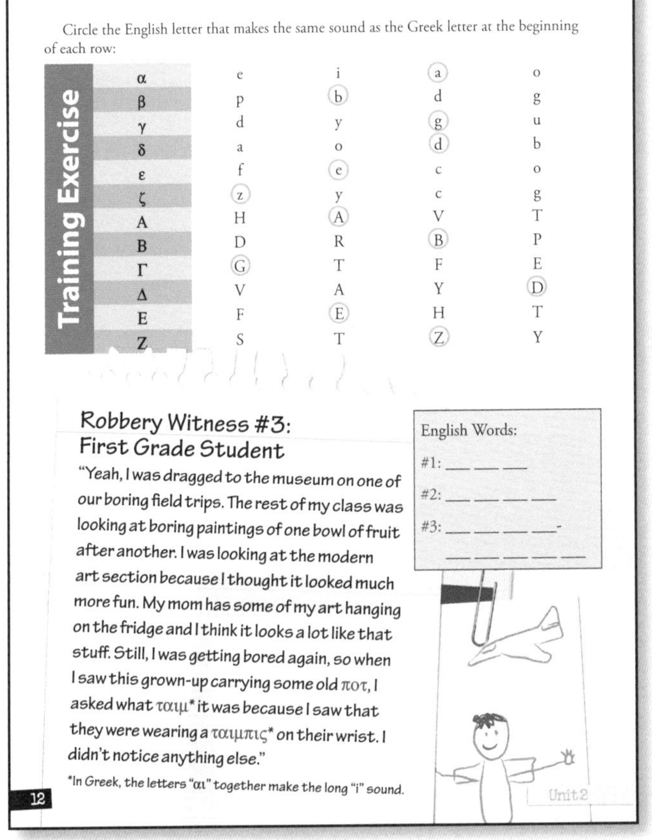

Circle the English letter that makes the same sound as the Greek letter at the beginning of each row:

Training Exercise

α	e	i	(a)	o
β	p	(b)	d	g
γ	d	y	(g)	u
δ	a	o	(d)	b
ε	f	(e)	c	o
ζ	(z)	y	c	g
A	H	(A)	V	T
B	D	R	(B)	P
Γ	(G)	T	F	E
Δ	V	A	Y	(D)
E	F	(E)	H	T
Z	S	T	(Z)	Y

Robbery Witness #3: First Grade Student

"Yeah, I was dragged to the museum on one of our boring field trips. The rest of my class was looking at boring paintings of one bowl of fruit after another. I was looking at the modern art section because I thought it looked much more fun. My mom has some of my art hanging on the fridge and I think it looks a lot like that stuff. Still, I was getting bored again, so when I saw this grown-up carrying some old ποτ, I asked what ταιμ* it was because I saw that they were wearing a ταιμπις* on their wrist. I didn't notice anything else."

*In Greek, the letters "αι" together make the long "i" sound.

English Words:
#1: ___
#2: ___
#3: ___

12

page 12

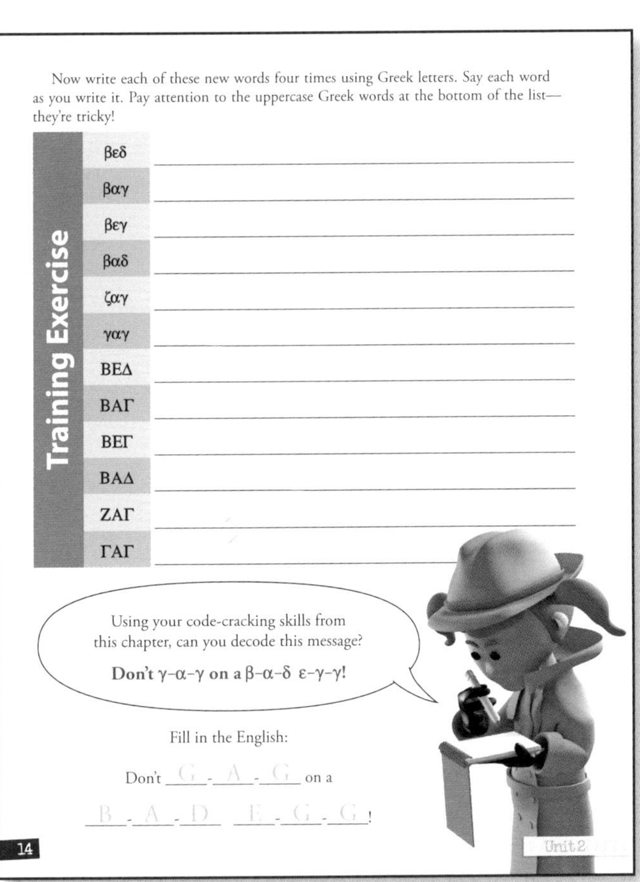

Now write each of these new words four times using Greek letters. Say each word as you write it. Pay attention to the uppercase Greek words at the bottom of the list—they're tricky!

Training Exercise

βεδ
βαγ
βεγ
βαδ
ζαγ
γαγ
ΒΕΔ
ΒΑΓ
ΒΕΓ
ΒΑΔ
ΖΑΓ
ΓΑΓ

Using your code-cracking skills from this chapter, can you decode this message?
Don't γ-α-γ on a β-α-δ ε-γ-γ!

Fill in the English:

Don't G - A - G on a B - A - D E - G - G!

14

page 14

Here are the answers for all the exercises throughout the book.

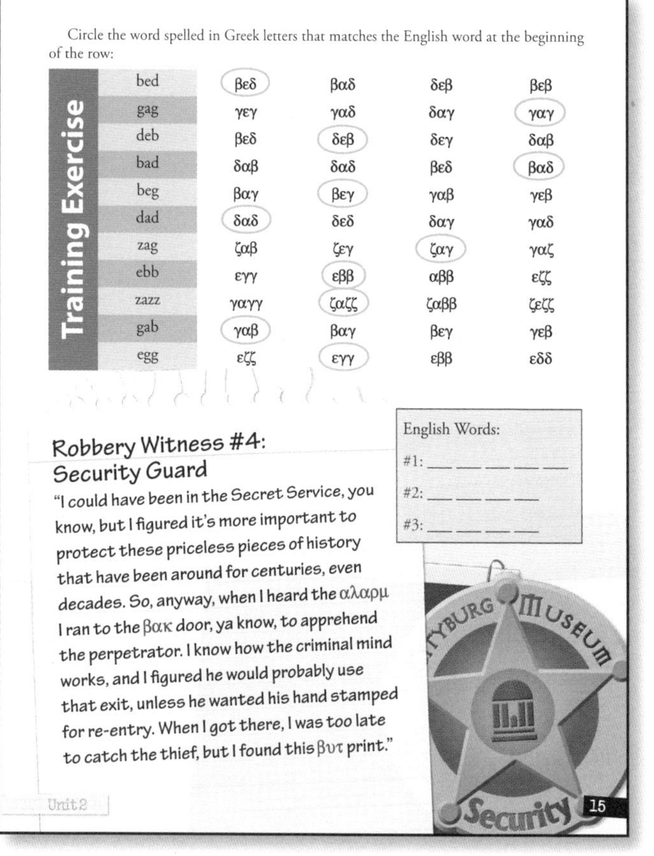

Circle the word spelled in Greek letters that matches the English word at the beginning of the row:

Training Exercise

bed	(βεδ)	βαδ	δεβ	βεβ
gag	γεγ	γαδ	δαγ	(γαγ)
deb	βεδ	(δεβ)	δεγ	δαβ
bad	δαβ	δαδ	βεδ	(βαδ)
beg	βαγ	(βεγ)	γαβ	γεβ
dad	(δαδ)	δεδ	δαγ	γαδ
zag	ζαβ	ζεγ	(ζαγ)	γαζ
ebb	εγγ	(εββ)	αββ	εζζ
zazz	γαγγ	(ζαζζ)	ζαββ	ζεζζ
gab	(γαβ)	βαγ	βεγ	γεβ
egg	εζζ	(εγγ)	εββ	εδδ

English Words:
#1: __ __ __ __ __
#2: __ __ __ __
#3: __ __ __ __

Robbery Witness #4: Security Guard

"I could have been in the Secret Service, you know, but I figured it's more important to protect these priceless pieces of history that have been around for centuries, even decades. So, anyway, when I heard the αλαρμ I ran to the βακ door, ya know, to apprehend the perpetrator. I know how the criminal mind works, and I figured he would probably use that exit, unless he wanted his hand stamped for re-entry. When I got there, I was too late to catch the thief, but I found this βυτ print."

Unit2 15

page 15

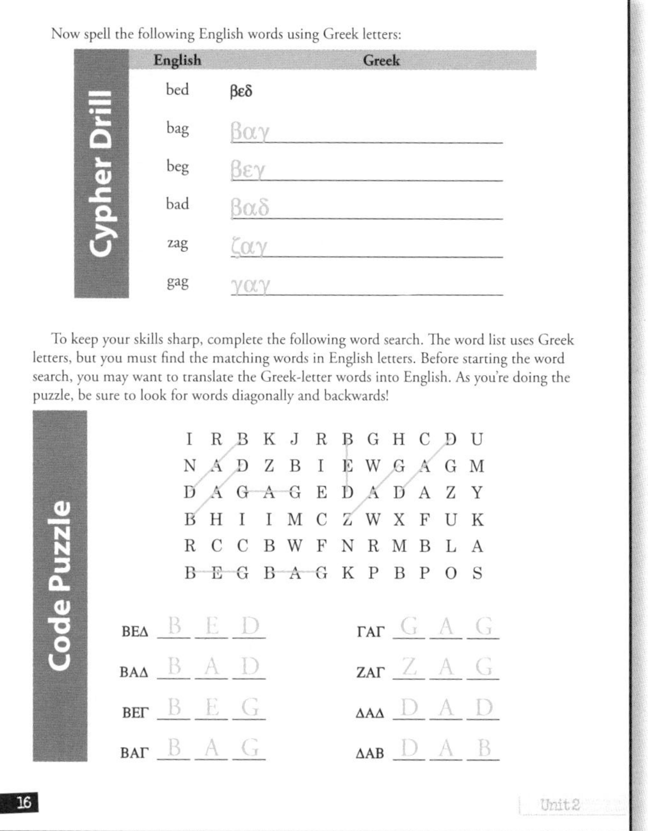

Now spell the following English words using Greek letters:

Cypher Drill

English	Greek
bed	βεδ
bag	βαγ
beg	βεγ
bad	βαδ
zag	ζαγ
gag	γαγ

To keep your skills sharp, complete the following word search. The word list uses Greek letters, but you must find the matching words in English letters. Before starting the word search, you may want to translate the Greek-letter words into English. As you're doing the puzzle, be sure to look for words diagonally and backwards!

Code Puzzle

```
I R B K J R B G H C D U
N A D Z B I E W G A G M
D A G A G E D A D A Z Y
B H I I M C Z W X F U K
R C C B W F N R M B L A
B E G B A G K P B P O S
```

ΒΕΔ	B E D	ΓΑΓ	G A G
ΒΑΔ	B A D	ΖΑΓ	Z A G
ΒΕΓ	B E G	ΔΑΔ	D A D
ΒΑΓ	B A G	ΔΑΒ	D A B

16 Unit2

page 16

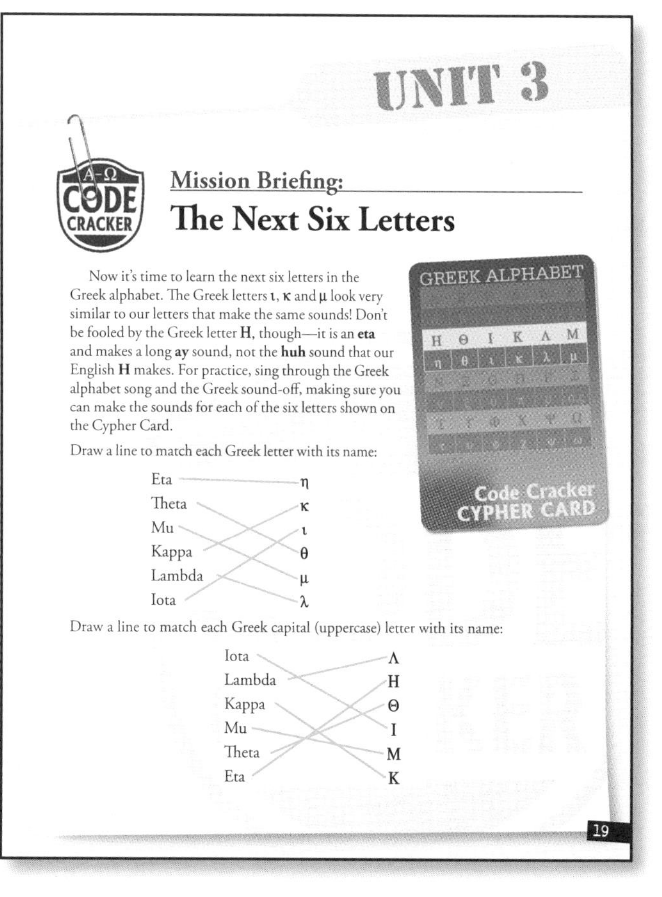

UNIT 3

Mission Briefing:

The Next Six Letters

Now it's time to learn the next six letters in the Greek alphabet. The Greek letters ι, κ and μ look very similar to our letters that make the same sounds! Don't be fooled by the Greek letter H, though—it is an **eta** and makes a long **ay** sound, not the **huh** sound that our English **H** makes. For practice, sing through the Greek alphabet song and the Greek sound-off, making sure you can make the sounds for each of the six letters shown on the Cypher Card.

Draw a line to match each Greek letter with its name:

Eta	η
Theta	κ
Mu	ι
Kappa	θ
Lambda	μ
Iota	λ

Draw a line to match each Greek capital (uppercase) letter with its name:

Iota	Λ
Lambda	H
Kappa	Θ
Mu	I
Theta	M
Eta	K

19

page 19

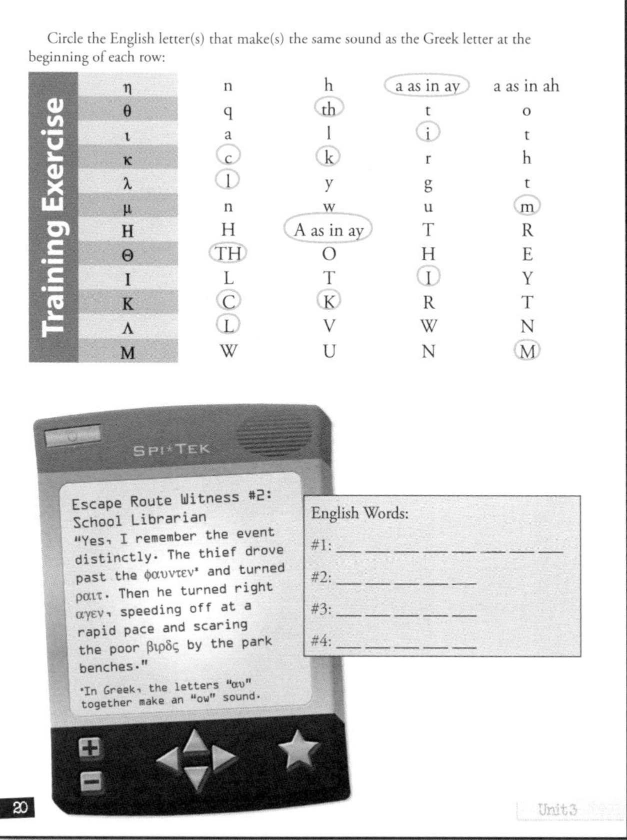

Circle the English letter(s) that make(s) the same sound as the Greek letter at the beginning of each row:

Training Exercise

η	n	h	(a as in ay)	a as in ah
θ	q	(th)	t	o
ι	a	l	(i)	t
κ	(c)	(k)	r	h
λ	(l)	y	g	t
μ	n	w	u	(m)
H	H	(A as in ay)	T	R
Θ	(TH)	O	H	E
I	L	T	(I)	Y
K	(C)	(K)	R	T
Λ	(L)	V	W	N
M	W	U	N	(M)

Escape Route Witness #2: School Librarian

"Yes, I remember the event distinctly. The thief drove past the φαυντεν* and turned ραιτ. Then he turned right αγεν, speeding off at a rapid pace and scaring the poor βιρδς by the park benches."

*In Greek, the letters "αυ" together make an "ow" sound.

English Words:
#1: __ __ __ __ __ __ __ __
#2: __ __ __ __ __
#3: __ __ __ __ __
#4: __ __ __ __ __

20 Unit3

page 20

Circle the word spelled in Greek letters that matches the English word at the beginning of the row:

Training Exercise

mad	μιδ	μαδ	μαγ	μαζ
bath	βεθ	βαβ	βαθ	θαβ
leg	γελ	ιεγ	λεγ	λαγ
bad	δαβ	δαδ	βεδ	βαδ
big	βαγ	βεγ	γιβ	βιγ
lag	λεγ	λαγ	γαλ	ιαγ
bake	βηκ	βακε	καβ	βικ
kid	κεδ	κιδ	κιγ	γιδ
zig	ζιβ	ζιζ	ζιγ	ζεγ
gab	γαβ	βαγ	βεγ	γεβ
Ellen	Ελλαν	Ελλεν	Ειιεν	Εγγεν

Now circle the English word that matches the Greek-letter word at the beginning of the row:

Training Exercise

μαδ	mid	mad	mag	maz
βαθ	beth	bab	bath	thab
λεγ	gel	ieg	leg	lag
βαδ	dab	dad	bed	bad
βιγ	bag	beg	gib	big
λαγ	leg	lag	gal	iag
βηκ	bak	bake	kab	bik
κιδ	ked	kid	kig	gid
ζιγ	zib	ziz	zig	zeg
γαβ	gab	bag	beg	geb
Εμμα	Enna	Ewwa	Euua	Emma

24 Unit3

page 24

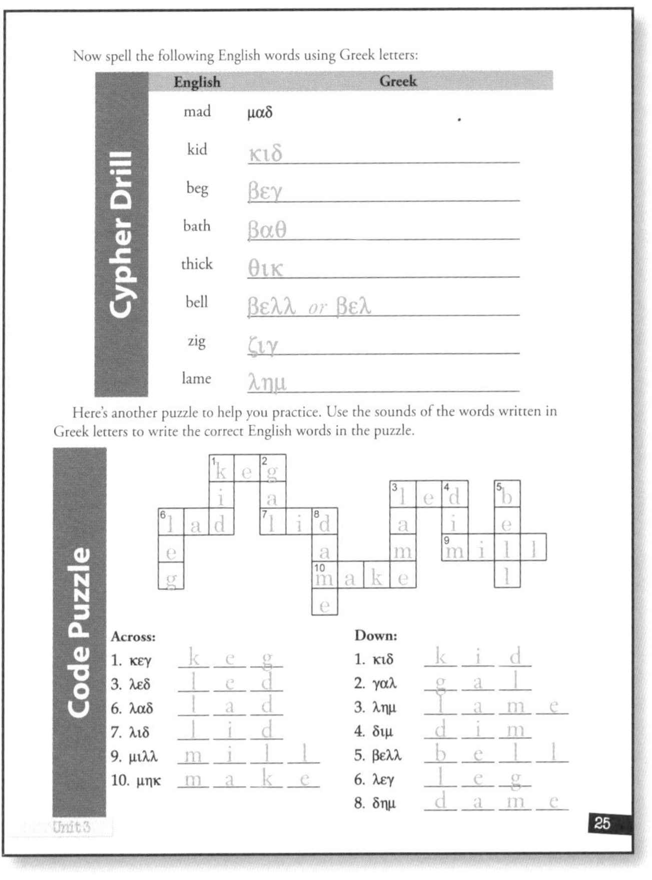

Now spell the following English words using Greek letters:

Cypher Drill

English	Greek
mad	μαδ
kid	κιδ
beg	βεγ
bath	βαθ
thick	θικ
bell	βελλ *or* βελ
zig	ζιγ
lame	λημ

Here's another puzzle to help you practice. Use the sounds of the words written in Greek letters to write the correct English words in the puzzle.

Code Puzzle

Across:
1. κεγ k e g
3. λεδ l e d
6. λαδ l a d
7. λιδ l i d
9. μιλλ m i l l
10. μηκ m a k e

Down:
1. κιδ k i d
2. γαλ g a l
3. λημ l a m e
4. διμ d i m
5. βελλ b e l l
6. λεγ l e g
8. δημ d a m e

Unit3 25

page 25

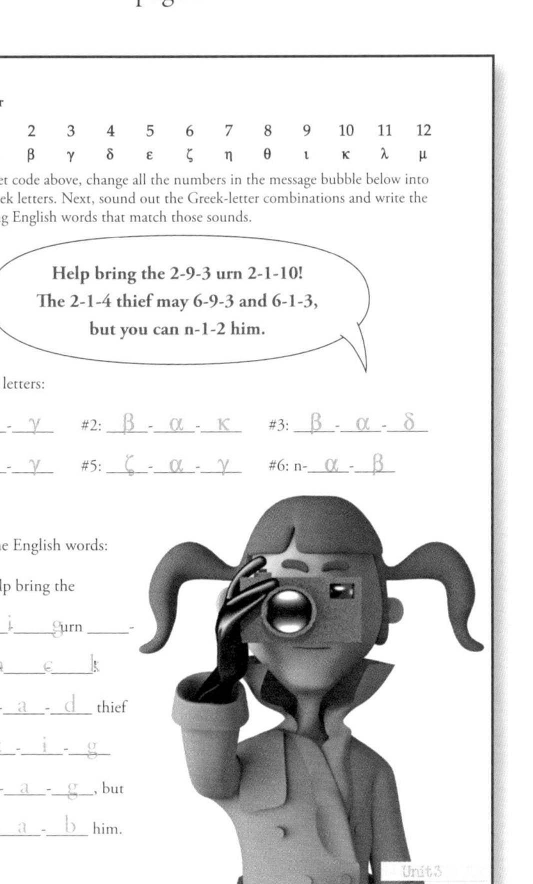

Two-Part Cypher

code	1	2	3	4	5	6	7	8	9	10	11	12
letter	α	β	γ	δ	ε	ζ	η	θ	ι	κ	λ	μ

Using the secret code above, change all the numbers in the message bubble below into the matching Greek letters. Next, sound out the Greek-letter combinations and write the final message using English words that match those sounds.

Help bring the 2-9-3 urn 2-1-10!
The 2-1-4 thief may 6-9-3 and 6-1-3,
but you can n-1-2 him.

Fill in the Greek letters:

#1: β - ι - γ #2: β - α - κ #3: β - α - δ

#4: ζ - ι - γ #5: ζ - α - γ #6: n- α - β

Fill in the English words:

Help bring the

b i g urn -

b a c k

The b - a - d thief

may z - i - g

and z - a - g, but

you can n- a - b him.

26 Unit3

page 26

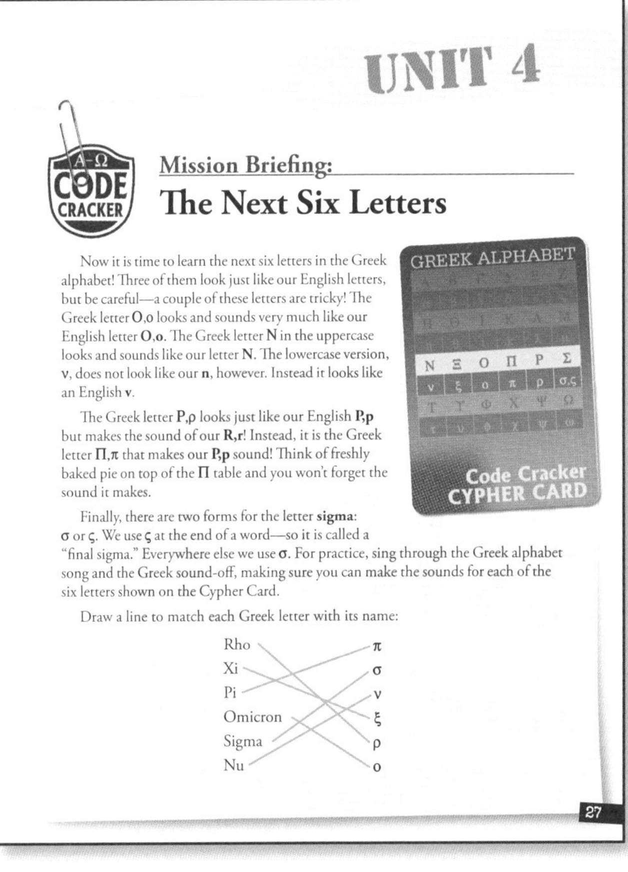

UNIT 4

Mission Briefing:
The Next Six Letters

Now it is time to learn the next six letters in the Greek alphabet! Three of them look just like our English letters, but be careful—a couple of these letters are tricky! The Greek letter **O,o** looks and sounds very much like our English letter **O,o**. The Greek letter **N** in the uppercase looks and sounds like our letter **N**. The lowercase version, **ν**, does not look like our **n**, however. Instead it looks like an English **v**.

The Greek letter **P,ρ** looks just like our English **P,p** but makes the sound of our **R,r**! Instead, it is the Greek letter **Π,π** that makes our **P,p** sound! Think of freshly baked pie on top of the **Π** table and you won't forget the sound it makes.

Finally, there are two forms for the letter **sigma**: σ or ς. We use ς at the end of a word—so it is called a "final sigma." Everywhere else we use σ. For practice, sing through the Greek alphabet song and the Greek sound-off, making sure you can make the sounds for each of the six letters shown on the Cypher Card.

Draw a line to match each Greek letter with its name:

Rho	π
Xi	σ
Pi	ν
Omicron	ξ
Sigma	ρ
Nu	ο

27

page 27

Draw a line to match each Greek capital (uppercase) letter with its name:

Name	Letter
Sigma	O
Nu	Ξ
Xi	N
Rho	Π
Omicron	Σ
Pi	P

Circle the English letter(s) that make(s) the same sound as the Greek letter at the beginning of each row:

Training Exercise

ν	w	v	(n)	h
ξ	b	s	e	(x)
ο	u	(o)	a	c
π	(p)	r	h	w
ρ	p	(r)	g	d
σ	o	(s)	c	a
N	(N)	V	W	L
Ξ	TH	(X)	H	E
O	C	D	(O)	G
Π	(P)	R	M	W
P	(R)	P	D	B
Σ	(S)	E	F	B

Combination Pepper Mill & Bug Detector

28 Unit 4

page 28

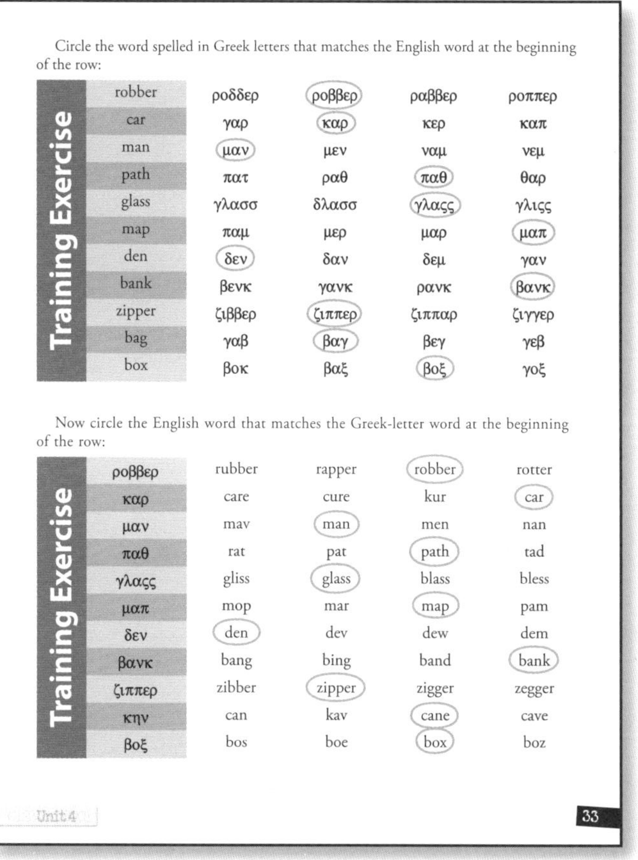
Circle the word spelled in Greek letters that matches the English word at the beginning of the row:

Training Exercise

robber	ροδδερ	(ροββερ)	ραββερ	ροππερ
car	γαρ	(καρ)	κερ	καπ
man	(μαν)	μεν	ναμ	νεμ
path	πατ	ραθ	(παθ)	θαρ
glass	γλασσ	δλασσ	(γλαςς)	γλιςς
map	παμ	μερ	μαρ	(μαπ)
den	(δεν)	δαν	δεμ	γαν
bank	βενκ	γανκ	ρανκ	(βανκ)
zipper	ζιββερ	(ζιππερ)	ζιππαρ	ζιγγερ
bag	γαβ	(βαγ)	βεγ	γεβ
box	βοκ	βαξ	(βοξ)	γοξ

Now circle the English word that matches the Greek-letter word at the beginning of the row:

Training Exercise

ροββερ	rubber	rapper	(robber)	rotter
καρ	care	cure	kur	(car)
μαν	mav	(man)	men	nan
παθ	rat	pat	(path)	tad
γλαςς	gliss	(glass)	blass	bless
μαπ	mop	mar	(map)	pam
δεν	(den)	dev	dew	dem
βανκ	bang	bing	band	(bank)
ζιππερ	zibber	(zipper)	zigger	zegger
κην	can	kav	(cane)	cave
βοξ	bos	boe	(box)	boz

Unit 4 33

page 33

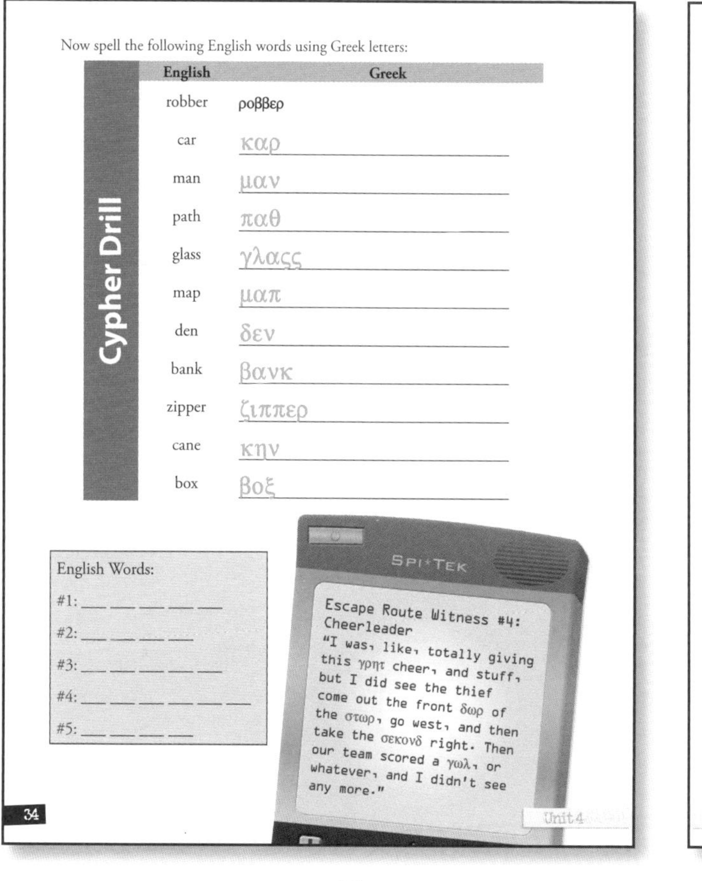
Now spell the following English words using Greek letters:

Cypher Drill

English	Greek
robber	ροββερ
car	καρ
man	μαν
path	παθ
glass	γλαςς
map	μαπ
den	δεν
bank	βανκ
zipper	ζιππερ
cane	κην
box	βοξ

English Words:
#1: ___ ___ ___ ___ ___
#2: ___ ___ ___ ___
#3: ___ ___ ___ ___ ___
#4: ___ ___ ___ ___ ___ ___
#5: ___ ___ ___ ___

SPI*TEK
Escape Route Witness #4: Cheerleader
"I was, like, totally giving this γρηt cheer, and stuff, but I did see the thief come out the front δωρ of the στωρ, go west, and then take the σεκονδ right. Then our team scored a γωλ, or whatever, and I didn't see any more."

34 Unit 4

page 34

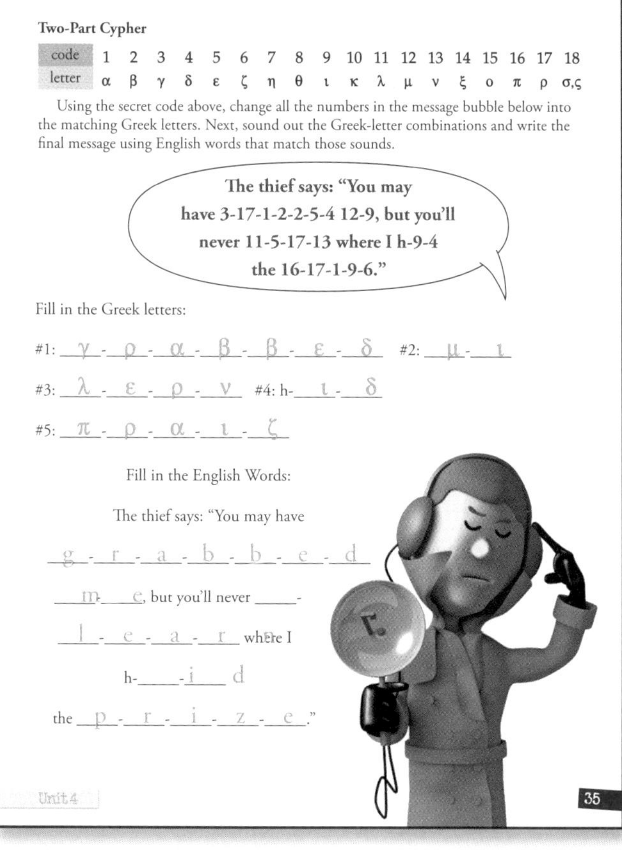
Two-Part Cypher

code	1	2	3	4	5	6	7	8	9	10	11	12	13	14	15	16	17	18
letter	α	β	γ	δ	ε	ζ	η	θ	ι	κ	λ	μ	ν	ξ	ο	π	ρ	σ,ς

Using the secret code above, change all the numbers in the message bubble below into the matching Greek letters. Next, sound out the Greek-letter combinations and write the final message using English words that match those sounds.

The thief says: "You may have 3-17-1-2-2-5-4 12-9, but you'll never 11-5-17-13 where I h-9-4 the 16-17-1-9-6."

Fill in the Greek letters:

#1: γ - ρ - α - β - β - ε - δ #2: μ - ι

#3: λ - ε - ρ - ν #4: h- ι - δ

#5: π - ρ - α - ι - ζ

Fill in the English Words:

The thief says: "You may have

g - r - a - b - b - e - d

m - e, but you'll never -

l - e - a - r - n where I

h- i - d

the p - r - i - z - e."

Unit 4 35

page 35

Here's another puzzle to help you practice. This time, use the provided English words to find the matching Greek-letter words. Be aware that some may be tricky because there may be more than one way to spell a matching word. Be sure to write out each of the English words in capital Greek letters before you try to solve the puzzle.

Code Puzzle

Β	Ρ	Ι	Κ	Υ	Μ	Θ	Ρ	Π	Τ	Λ	Υ
Α	Δ	Γ	Κ	Υ	Α	Α	Α	Χ	Ο	Β	Β
Ρ	Ω	Ν	Ε	Π	Ν	Α	Ν	Π	Ν	Δ	Ρ
Δ	Α	Π	Ο	Π	Κ	Σ	Α	Ρ	Τ	Ε	Φ
Β	Ο	Ρ	Δ	Δ	Ε	Μ	Ν	Ν	Υ	Ν	Ν
Υ	Α	Λ	Ρ	Ρ	Ι	Π	Η	Ο	Τ	Ρ	Υ
Β	Ο	Ξ	Ε	Ρ	Α	Κ	Κ	Ν	Ρ	Ν	Η
Ν	Κ	Κ	Σ	Ν	Κ	Ν	Α	Φ	Ν	Π	Υ
Φ	Υ	Δ	Λ	Α	Υ	Λ	Ρ	Α	Α	Μ	Γ
Μ	Λ	Ξ	Ρ	Μ	Ε	Β	Π	Ν	Β	Ρ	Β
Τ	Θ	Ω	Χ	Ι	Ο	Τ	Β	Α	Τ	Ω	Ν
Β	Α	Π	Ω	Τ	Λ	Υ	Κ	Δ	Τ	Ε	Λ

CAR Κ Α Ρ — BOX Β Ο Ξ

MAN Μ Α Ν — BOXER Β Ο Ξ Ε Ρ

PATH Π Α Θ — NAP Ν Α Π

RAN Ρ Α Ν — RACK Ρ Α Κ

PAN Π Α Ν — COB Χ Ο Β

MAP Μ Α Π — BRICK Β Ρ Ι Κ

DEN Δ Ε Ν — CLAP Κ Λ Α Π

BANK Β Α Ν Κ — CAB Κ Α Β

CANE Κ Η Ν — POP Π Ο Π

page 36

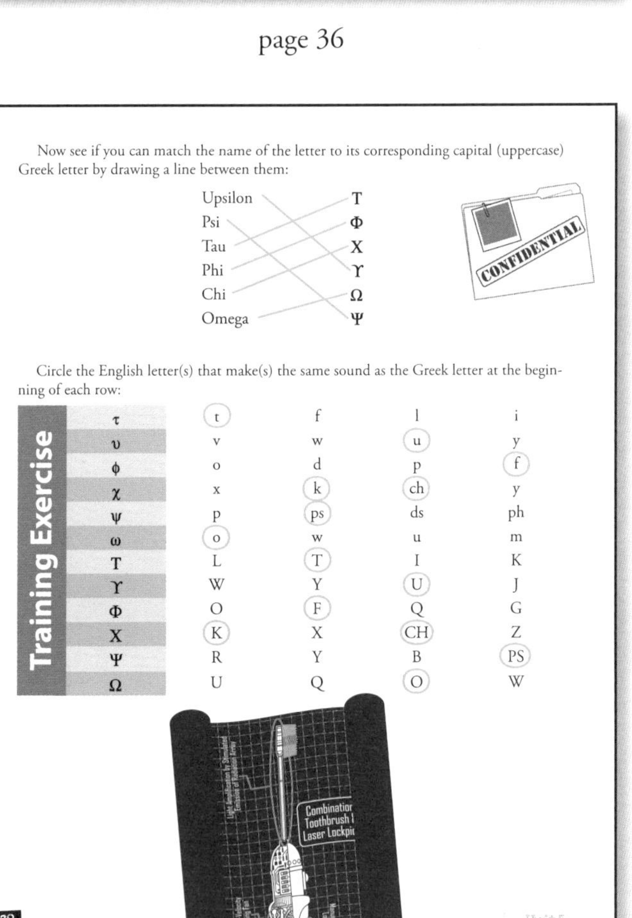

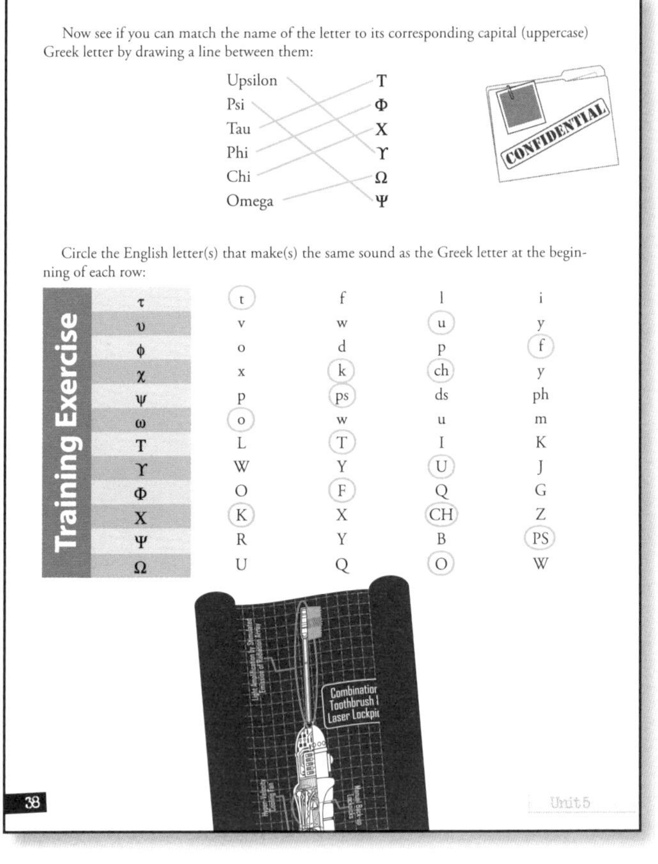

UNIT 5

Mission Briefing:
The Last Six Letters

Now it's time to learn the last six letters of the Greek alphabet! Just like before, there are a few letters in this group that look and sound like our English letters and there are also a couple of tricky ones.

Let's look at the tricky ones first. The uppercase **upsilon**—Υ—may look like our English **Y**, but it sounds like our **u**, as in **glue**! Remember, there is no Greek **y**. The Greek letter **Χ,χ** looks just like our **X,x** but it really makes the sound of our English **k**, a hard **c** (as in **cat**), or a **ch** (as in **chorus**). The Greek letter **ω** looks like our **w** but it makes the sound of a long **o** (as in **bone**).

The Greek letter **Τ,τ** is an easy one, since it looks and sounds like our **T,t**. In contrast, the letters **Φ,φ**, **Ψ,ψ**, and **Ω,ω** are unlike any of our English letters, but they sure are strange and fun!

For practice, sing through the Greek alphabet song and the Greek alphabet sound-off, making sure you can make the sounds for each of the six letters shown on the Cypher Card.

Draw a line to match each Greek letter with its name:

Omega	ψ
Chi	ω
Phi	υ
Tau	χ
Psi	φ
Upsilon	τ

page 37

Now see if you can match the name of the letter to its corresponding capital (uppercase) Greek letter by drawing a line between them:

Upsilon	Τ
Psi	Φ
Tau	Χ
Phi	Υ
Chi	Ω
Omega	Ψ

Circle the English letter(s) that make(s) the same sound as the Greek letter at the beginning of each row:

Training Exercise

τ	(t)	f	l	i
υ	v	w	(u)	y
φ	o	d	p	(f)
χ	x	(k)	(ch)	y
ψ	p	(ps)	ds	ph
ω	(o)	w	u	m
Τ	L	(T)	I	K
Υ	W	Y	(U)	J
Φ	O	(F)	Q	G
Χ	(K)	X	(CH)	Z
Ψ	R	Y	B	(PS)
Ω	U	Q	(O)	W

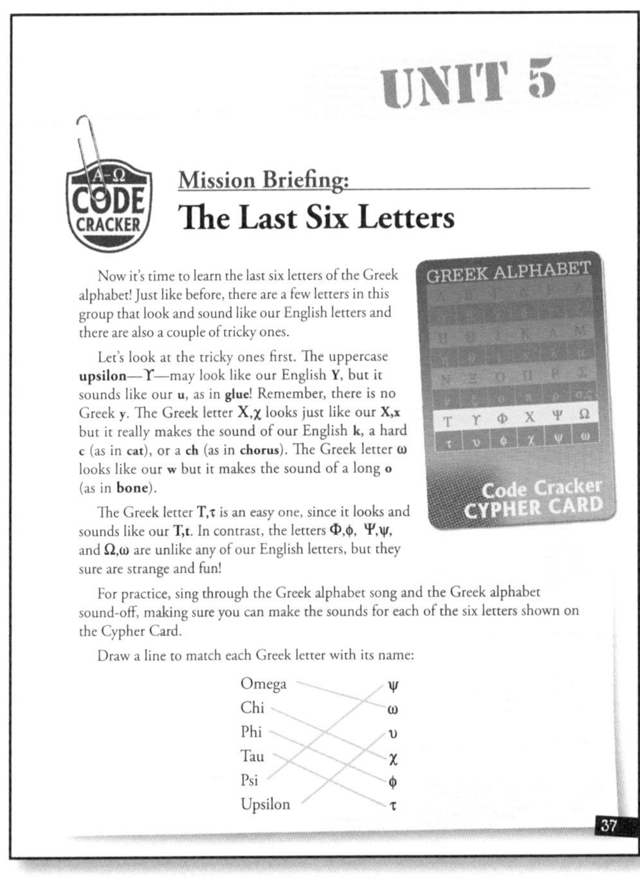

page 38

Circle the word spelled in Greek letters that matches the English word at the beginning of the row:

Training Exercise

new	νεω	(νυ)	νοω	νω
art	απε	απτ	(αρτ)	ταρ
clue	κυλ	(κλυ)	κλω	κλε
bad	βιδ	δαβ	(βαδ)	βαρ
gob	γοδ	δογ	γααδ	(γοβ)
broken	βροκεν	βρωκερ	(βρωκεν)	βρωτεν
in	εν	ιμ	(ιν)	ον
road	(ρωδ)	ροδ	δορ	δωρ
street	στιτ	(στριτ)	στικτ	στεεπ
forbidden	φορβιττεν	φαρβιττεν	φορβικκεν	(φορβιδδεν)
moon	μυμ	μον	μυω	(μυν)
all	αιι	ακκ	(αλλ)	αττ
free	φριι	φρεε	φρυ	(φρι)

English Words:

#1: ___ ___ ___ ___ ___

#2: ___ ___ ___

#3: ___ ___ ___ ___

#4: ___ ___ ___ ___ ___

#5: ___ ___ ___ ___

SPI TEK

Escape Route Witness #5:
Helicopter Pilot
"I was busy showing this new παιλοτ the ropes when I noticed the speeding χαρ. It took the first λεφτ, then turned wildly again and headed νορθ. The driver seemed like he was going very φαστ."

page 43

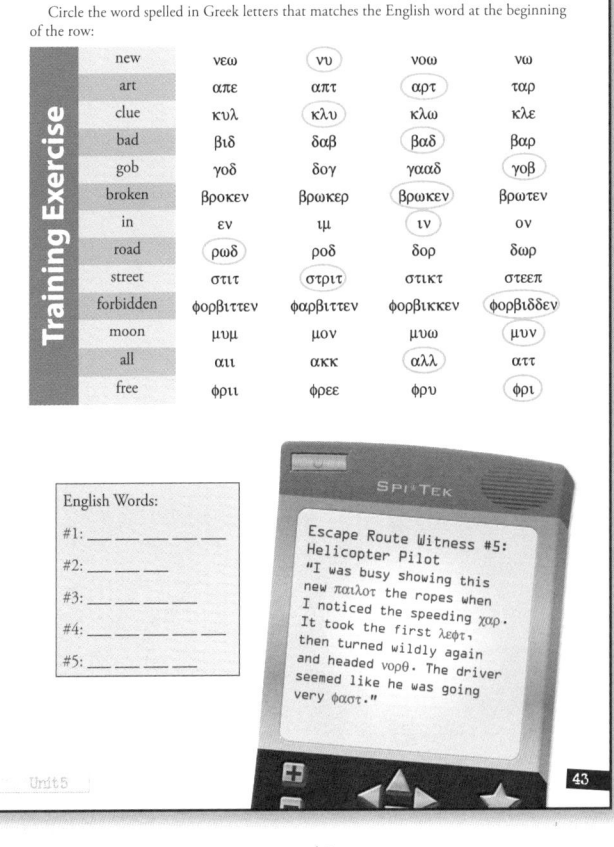

Now circle the English word that matches the Greek-letter word at the beginning of the row:

Training Exercise

Greek				
νυ	no	neo	(new)	knee
αρτ	urp	arm	ark	(art)
κλυ	glue	klu	(clue)	crew
βαδ	bid	bud	dad	(bad)
γοβ	gab	bug	(gob)	gut
βρωκεν	brick	brake	shaken	(broken)
ιν	on	it	(in)	un
ρωδ	ride	rope	(road)	read
στριτ	stick	strap	strict	(street)
φορβιδδεν	forbitten	(forbidden)	farbidden	forbikken
μυν	man	muck	mean	(moon)
αλλ	ill	al	(all)	at
φρι	fry	(free)	from	fro

Now spell the following English words using Greek letters:

Cypher Drill

English	Greek
new	νυ
art	αρτ
clue	κλυ *or* χλυ
bad	βαδ
gob	γοβ
broken	βρωκεν
in	ιν

page 44

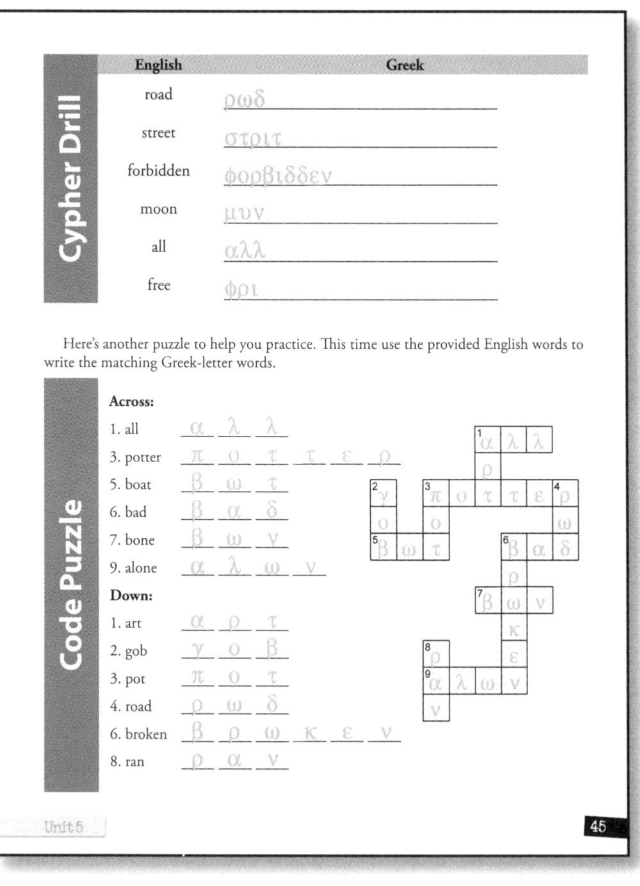

Cypher Drill

English	Greek
road	ρωδ
street	στριτ
forbidden	φορβιδδεν
moon	μυν
all	αλλ
free	φρι

Here's another puzzle to help you practice. This time use the provided English words to write the matching Greek-letter words.

Code Puzzle

Across:

1. all α λ λ
3. potter π ο τ τ ε ρ
5. boat β ω τ
6. bad β α δ
7. bone β ω ν
9. alone α λ ω ν

Down:

1. art α ρ τ
2. gob γ ο β
3. pot π ο τ
4. road ρ ω δ
6. broken β ρ ω κ ε ν
8. ran ρ α ν

Unit5 45

page 45

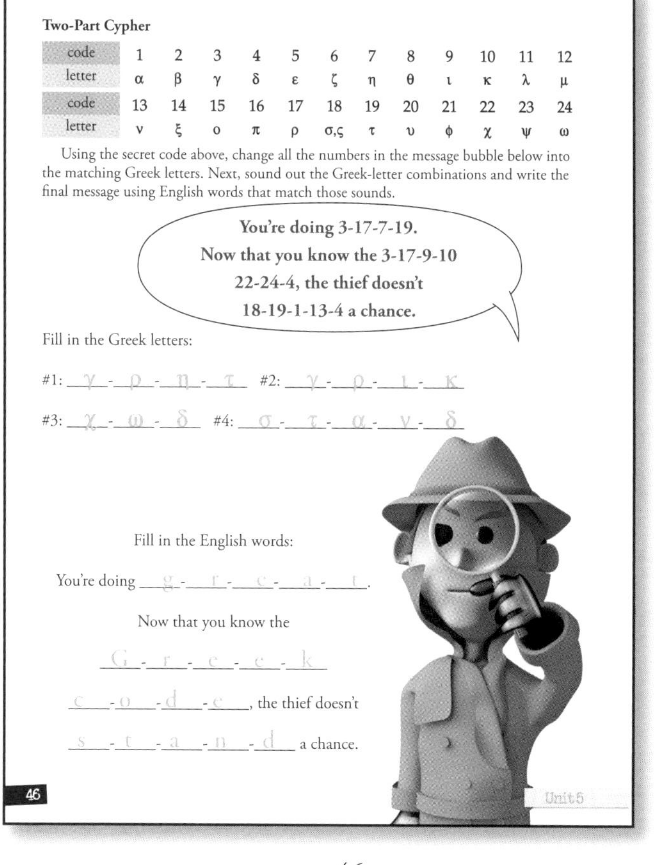

Two-Part Cypher

code	1	2	3	4	5	6	7	8	9	10	11	12
letter	α	β	γ	δ	ε	ζ	η	θ	ι	κ	λ	μ
code	13	14	15	16	17	18	19	20	21	22	23	24
letter	ν	ξ	ο	π	ρ	σ,ς	τ	υ	φ	χ	ψ	ω

Using the secret code above, change all the numbers in the message bubble below into the matching Greek letters. Next, sound out the Greek-letter combinations and write the final message using English words that match those sounds.

You're doing 3-17-7-19.
Now that you know the 3-17-9-10
22-24-4, the thief doesn't
18-19-1-13-4 a chance.

Fill in the Greek letters:

#1: γ - ρ - η - τ #2: γ - ρ - ι - κ

#3: χ - ω - δ #4: σ - τ - α - ν - δ

Fill in the English words:

You're doing g - r - e - a - t.

Now that you know the

G - r - e - e - k

c - o - d - e, the thief doesn't

s - t - a - n - d a chance.

46 Unit5

page 46

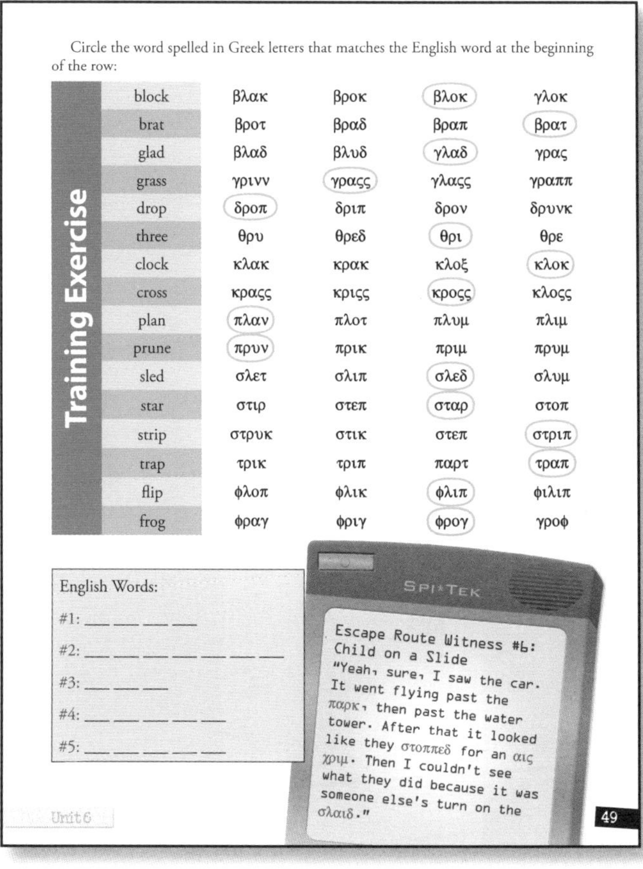

Circle the word spelled in Greek letters that matches the English word at the beginning of the row:

Training Exercise

English				
block	βλακ	βροκ	(βλοκ)	γλοκ
brat	βροτ	βραδ	βραπ	(βρατ)
glad	βλαδ	βλυδ	(γλαδ)	γρας
grass	γριvv	(γραςς)	γλαςς	γραππ
drop	(δροπ)	δριπ	δρον	δρυνκ
three	θρυ	θρεδ	(θρι)	θρε
clock	κλακ	κρακ	κλοξ	(κλοκ)
cross	κραςς	κριςς	(κροςς)	κλοςς
plan	(πλαν)	πλοτ	πλυμ	πλιμ
prune	(πρυν)	πρικ	πριμ	πρυμ
sled	σλετ	σλιπ	(σλεδ)	σλυμ
star	στιρ	στεπ	(σταρ)	στοπ
strip	στρυκ	στικ	στεπ	(στριπ)
trap	τρικ	τριπ	παρτ	(τραπ)
flip	φλοπ	φλικ	(φλιπ)	φιλιπ
frog	φραγ	φριγ	(φρογ)	γροφ

English Words:

#1: ____
#2: ________
#3: ___
#4: _____
#5: _____

SPI TEK
Escape Route Witness #6:
Child on a Slide
"Yeah, sure, I saw the car.
It went flying past the
παρκ, then past the water
tower. After that it looked
like they στοππεδ for an αις
κριμ. Then I couldn't see
what they did because it was
someone else's turn on the
σλαιδ."

Unit6 49

page 49

Now circle the English word that matches the Greek-letter word at the beginning of the row:

Training Exercise

βλοκ	black	(block)	blip	blot
βρατ	bret	brick	(brat)	brad
γλαδ	(glad)	glass	blood	glop
γρας	gram	grin	(grass)	grape
δροπ	drip	drum	drat	(drop)
θρι	the	(three)	threw	free
κλοκ	cluck	click	(clock)	clack
κρος	chris	crass	cron	(cross)
πλαν	plum	(plan)	plus	plot
πρυν	(prune)	prim	prick	prod
σλεδ	slot	slet	slip	(sled)
σταρ	store	(star)	stir	stap
στριπ	stick	step	(strip)	strep
τραπ	part	(trap)	track	trip
φλιπ	flick	flop	lips	(flip)
φρογ	frag	(frog)	frig	froy

English Words:
#1: ___ ___ ___ ___ ___
#2: ___ ___ ___ ___
#3: ___ ___ ___ ___ ___ ___ ___
#4: ___ ___ ___ ___
#5: ___ ___ ___

SPI*TEK

Escape Route Witness #7:
Gas Station Attendant
"I saw the thief drive right by our σταρ. He then turned and stopped at the dock by the λαμπ, renting a παδδελ βωτ. You should have seen him working like crazy to move that thing, especially with that βιγ jar he had."

50 Unit6

page 50

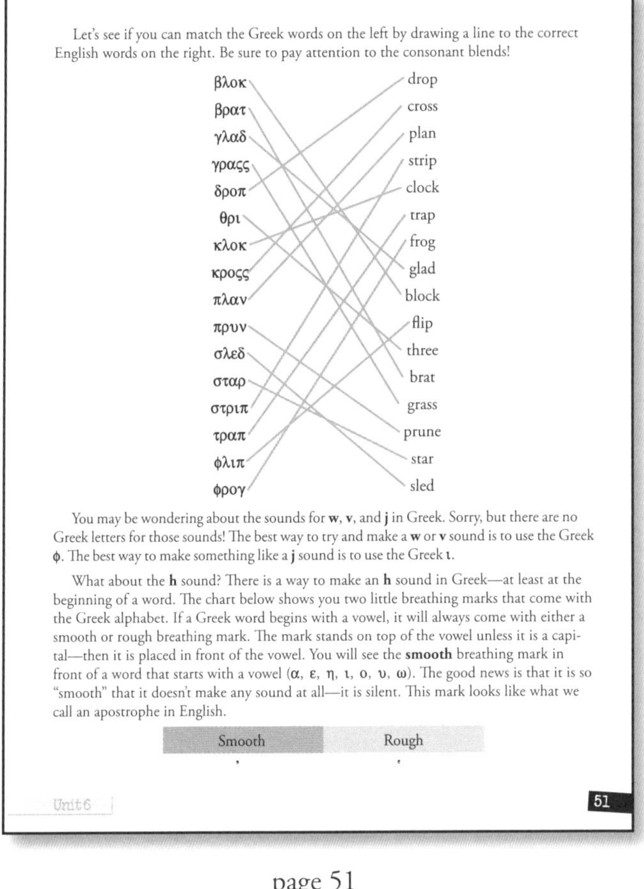

Let's see if you can match the Greek words on the left by drawing a line to the correct English words on the right. Be sure to pay attention to the consonant blends!

Greek	English
βλοκ	drop
βρατ	cross
γλαδ	plan
γρας	strip
δροπ	clock
θρι	trap
κλοκ	frog
κρος	glad
πλαν	block
πρυν	flip
σλεδ	three
σταρ	brat
στριπ	grass
τραπ	prune
φλιπ	star
φρογ	sled

You may be wondering about the sounds for **w**, **v**, and **j** in Greek. Sorry, but there are no Greek letters for those sounds! The best way to try and make a **w** or **v** sound is to use the Greek φ. The best way to make something like a **j** sound is to use the Greek ι.

What about the **h** sound? There is a way to make an **h** sound in Greek—at least at the beginning of a word. The chart below shows you two little breathing marks that come with the Greek alphabet. If a Greek word begins with a vowel, it will always come with either a smooth or rough breathing mark. The mark stands on top of the vowel unless it is a capital—then it is placed in front of the vowel. You will see the **smooth** breathing mark in front of a word that starts with a vowel (α, ε, η, ι, ο, υ, ω). The good news is that it is so "smooth" that it doesn't make any sound at all—it is silent. This mark looks like what we call an apostrophe in English.

Smooth	Rough
ʼ	ʽ

Unit6 51

page 51

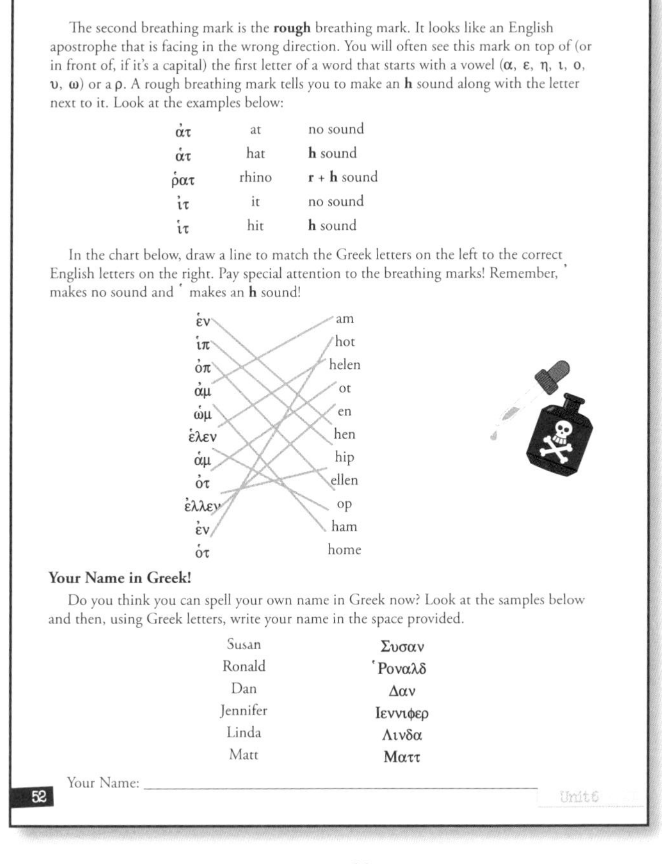

The second breathing mark is the **rough** breathing mark. It looks like an English apostrophe that is facing in the wrong direction. You will often see this mark on top of (or in front of, if it's a capital) the first letter of a word that starts with a vowel (α, ε, η, ι, ο, υ, ω) or a ρ. A rough breathing mark tells you to make an **h** sound along with the letter next to it. Look at the examples below:

ἀτ	at	no sound
ἁτ	hat	**h** sound
ῥατ	rhino	**r** + **h** sound
ἰτ	it	no sound
ἱτ	hit	**h** sound

In the chart below, draw a line to match the Greek letters on the left to the correct English letters on the right. Pay special attention to the breathing marks! Remember, ʼ makes no sound and ʽ makes an **h** sound!

Greek	English
ἐν	am
ἱπ	hot
ὀπ	helen
ἀμ	ot
ὡμ	en
ἑλεν	hen
ἁμ	hip
ὁτ	ellen
ἐλλεν	op
ἑν	ham
ὀτ	home

Your Name in Greek!

Do you think you can spell your own name in Greek now? Look at the samples below and then, using Greek letters, write your name in the space provided.

Susan	Συσαν
Ronald	ʽΡοναλδ
Dan	Δαν
Jennifer	Ιεννιφερ
Linda	Λινδα
Matt	Ματτ

Your Name: ______________________

52 Unit6

page 52

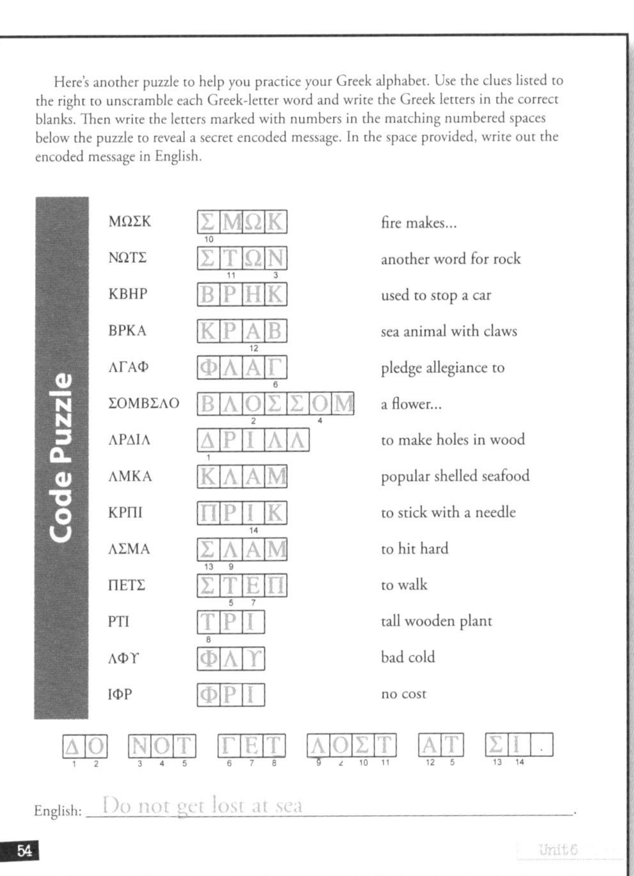

Here's another puzzle to help you practice your Greek alphabet. Use the clues listed to the right to unscramble each Greek-letter word and write the Greek letters in the correct blanks. Then write the letters marked with numbers in the matching numbered spaces below the puzzle to reveal a secret encoded message. In the space provided, write out the encoded message in English.

Code Puzzle

Scrambled	Answer	Clue
ΜΩΣΚ	ΣΜΩΚ	fire makes...
ΝΩΤΣ	ΣΤΩΝ	another word for rock
ΚΒΗΡ	ΒΡΗΚ	used to stop a car
ΒΡΚΑ	ΚΡΑΒ	sea animal with claws
ΛΓΑΦ	ΦΛΑΓ	pledge allegiance to
ΣΟΜΒΣΛΟ	ΒΛΟΣΣΟΜ	a flower...
ΑΡΔΙΛ	ΔΡΙΛΛ	to make holes in wood
ΛΜΚΑ	ΚΛΑΜ	popular shelled seafood
ΚΡΠΙ	ΠΡΙΚ	to stick with a needle
ΛΣΜΑ	ΣΛΑΜ	to hit hard
ΠΕΤΣ	ΣΤΕΠ	to walk
ΡΤΙ	ΤΡΙ	tall wooden plant
ΛΦΥ	ΦΛΥ	bad cold
ΙΦΡ	ΦΡΙ	no cost

ΔΟ ΝΟΤ ΓΕΤ ΛΟΣΤ ΑΤ ΣΙ.

English: Do not get lost at sea.

54 Unit6

page 54

Now draw a line to match the Greek-letter word on the left with the correct English word on the right:

τεικ	weed
υιδ	about
ρουμ	take
υι	boil
βαικ	few
βοιλ	room
αβαυτ	wee
φευ	bike

English Words:

#1: __ __ __ __ __ __ __ __

#2: __ __ __ __ __ __

#3: __ __ __ __ __

#4: __ __ __ __

#5: __ __ __ __ __ __ __

SPI-TEK

Escape Route Witness #8:
Dock Worker
"After several attempts at waterskiing, the thief gave up and docked at the pier by the βιγεστ beach--the one near the τριç. He hot-wired a πιζζα truck and headed βακ toward the σεντερ of town."

Unit7 57

page 57

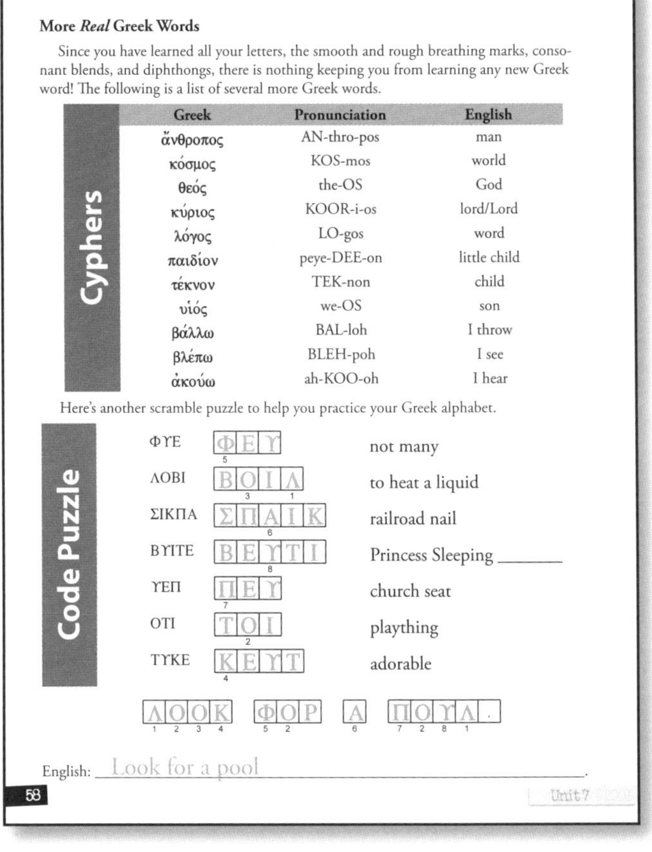

More *Real* Greek Words

Since you have learned all your letters, the smooth and rough breathing marks, consonant blends, and diphthongs, there is nothing keeping you from learning any new Greek word! The following is a list of several more Greek words.

Cyphers

Greek	Pronunciation	English
ἄνθρωπος	AN-thro-pos	man
κόσμος	KOS-mos	world
θεός	the-OS	God
κύριος	KOOR-i-os	lord/Lord
λόγος	LO-gos	word
παιδίον	peye-DEE-on	little child
τέκνον	TEK-non	child
υἱός	we-OS	son
βάλλω	BAL-loh	I throw
βλέπω	BLEH-poh	I see
ἀκούω	ah-KOO-oh	I hear

Here's another scramble puzzle to help you practice your Greek alphabet.

Code Puzzle

ΦΥΕ	ΦΕΥ (5)	not many
ΛΟΒΙ	ΒΟΙΛ (3, 1)	to heat a liquid
ΣΙΚΠΑ	ΣΠΑΙΚ (6)	railroad nail
ΒΥΙΤΕ	ΒΕΥΤΙ (8)	Princess Sleeping ______
ΥΕΠ	ΠΕΥ (7)	church seat
ΟΤΙ	ΤΟΙ (2)	plaything
ΤΥΚΕ	ΚΕΥΤ (4)	adorable

ΛΟΟΚ ΦΟΡ Α ΠΟΥΛ.

English: Look for a pool.

58 Unit7

page 58

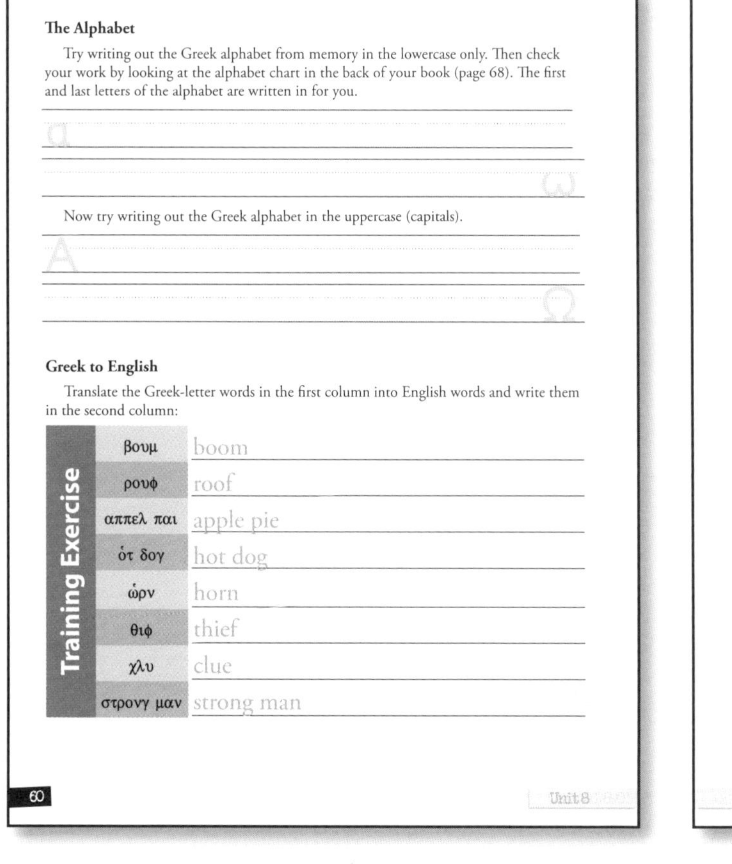

The Alphabet

Try writing out the Greek alphabet from memory in the lowercase only. Then check your work by looking at the alphabet chart in the back of your book (page 68). The first and last letters of the alphabet are written in for you.

α ... ω

Now try writing out the Greek alphabet in the uppercase (capitals).

Α ... Ω

Greek to English

Translate the Greek-letter words in the first column into English words and write them in the second column:

Training Exercise

βουμ	boom
ρουφ	roof
απελ παι	apple pie
ὁτ δογ	hot dog
ὡρν	horn
θιφ	thief
χλυ	clue
στρονγ μαν	strong man

60 Unit8

page 60

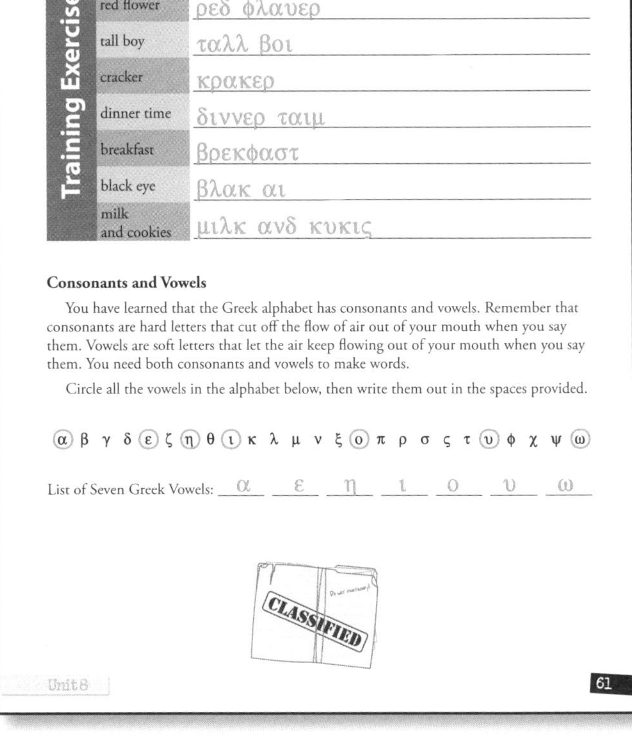

Translate the English words in the first column into Greek-letter words and write them in the second column:

Training Exercise

stray cat	στρη κατ
red flower	ρεδ φλαυερ
tall boy	ταλλ βοι
cracker	κρακερ
dinner time	διννερ ταιμ
breakfast	βρεκφαστ
black eye	βλακ αι
milk and cookies	μιλκ ανδ κυκις

Consonants and Vowels

You have learned that the Greek alphabet has consonants and vowels. Remember that consonants are hard letters that cut off the flow of air out of your mouth when you say them. Vowels are soft letters that let the air keep flowing out of your mouth when you say them. You need both consonants and vowels to make words.

Circle all the vowels in the alphabet below, then write them out in the spaces provided.

(α) β γ δ (ε) ζ (η) θ (ι) κ λ μ ν ξ (ο) π ρ σ ς τ (υ) φ χ ψ (ω)

List of Seven Greek Vowels: α ε η ι ο υ ω

CLASSIFIED

Unit8 61

page 61

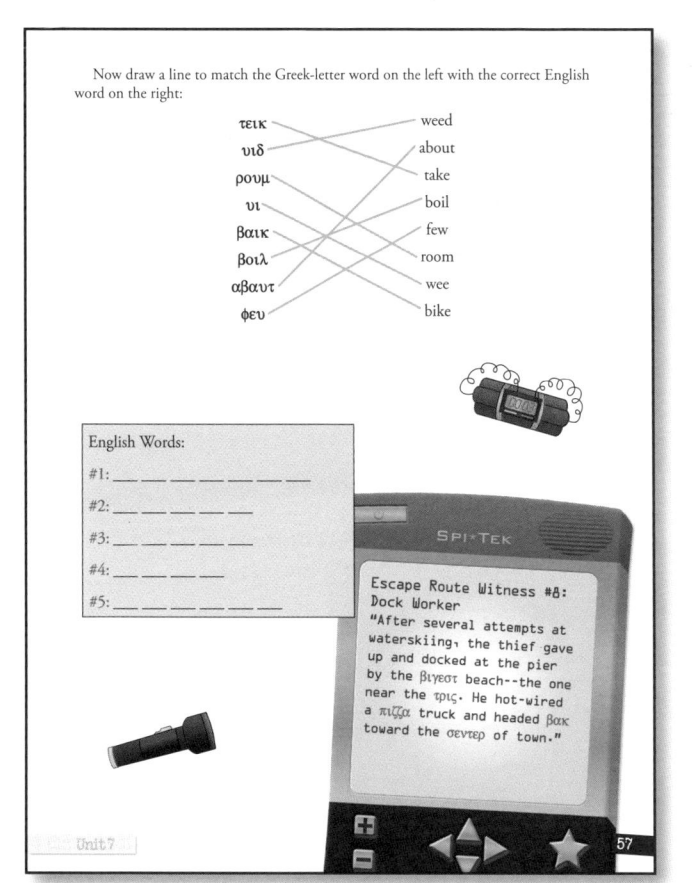

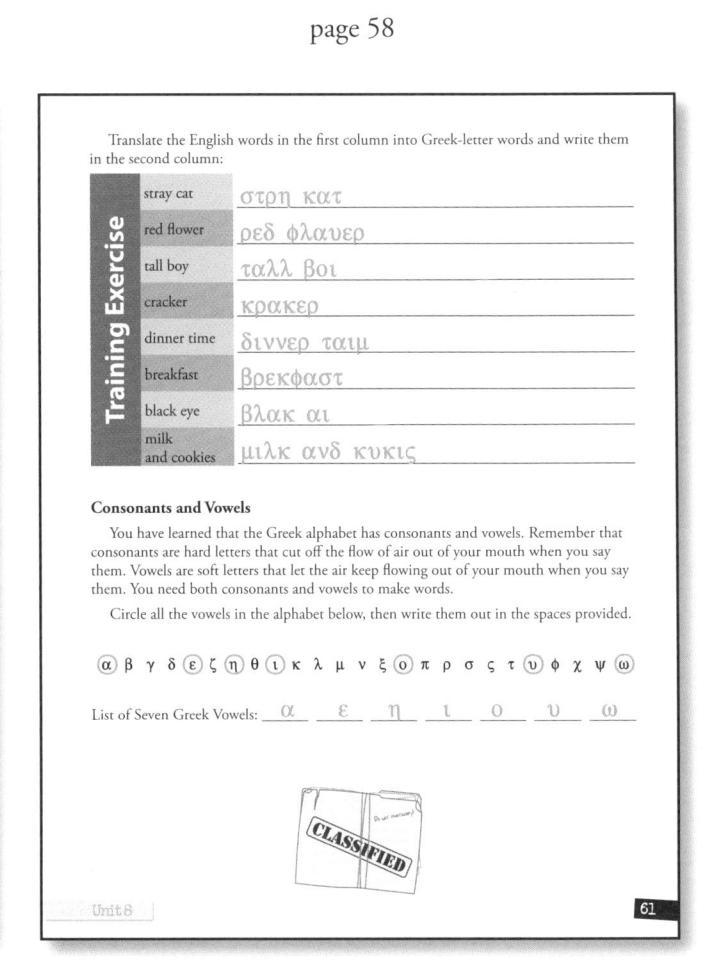

Blends and Diphthongs

Once you remove all six of the vowels from the Greek alphabet, you have eighteen letters left, and they are all consonants. There are several ways that you can blend consonants together to make "blended" sounds. The following are several Greek-letter words that have blends. Underline the blended Greek letters, then write out the English word and underline the blended English letters.

Cypher Drill

Greek	English	Greek	English
πρυν	prune	σλεδ	sled
βραν	bran	σταρ	star
γλοβ	glob	στριπ	strip
γριν	grin	τρομβων	trombone
δροπ	drop	φλιπ	flip
θρι	three	φρογ	frog
κλαπ	clap	σλιμ	slim
κρισπ	crisp	βλεςς	bless
πλαν	plan	κρυδ	crude
βλυ	blue	γλιττερ	glitter

SPI*TEK

Escape Route Witness #9:
Lifeguard at the Πουλ
"Dude, the truck drove past us, then turned λεφτ. Then I was like 'whoa!' because it took the first λεφτ and went παστ us on the οθερ side and then turned right."

English Words:
#1: ___ ___ ___ ___
#2: ___ ___ ___ ___
#3: ___ ___ ___ ___
#4: ___ ___ ___ ___
#5: ___ ___ ___ ___ ___

62 Unit 8

page 62

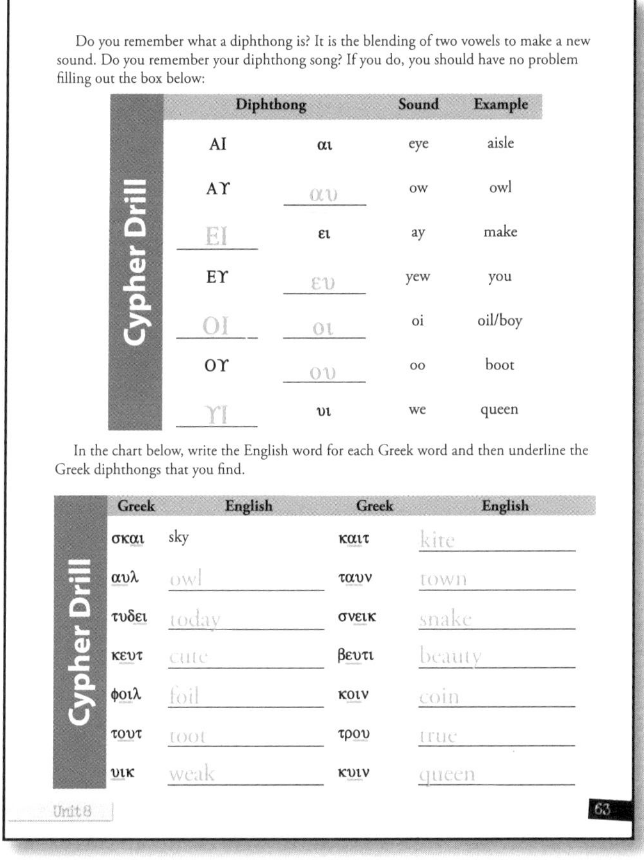

Do you remember what a diphthong is? It is the blending of two vowels to make a new sound. Do you remember your diphthong song? If you do, you should have no problem filling out the box below:

Cypher Drill

Diphthong		Sound	Example
AI	αι	eye	aisle
AΥ	αυ	ow	owl
EI	ει	ay	make
EΥ	ευ	yew	you
OI	οι	oi	oil/boy
OΥ	ου	oo	boot
ΥI	υι	we	queen

In the chart below, write the English word for each Greek word and then underline the Greek diphthongs that you find.

Greek	English	Greek	English
σκαι	sky	καιτ	kite
αυλ	owl	ταυν	town
τυδει	today	σνεικ	snake
κευτ	cute	βευτι	beauty
φοιλ	foil	κοιν	coin
τουτ	toot	τρου	true
υικ	weak	κυιν	queen

Unit 8 63

page 63

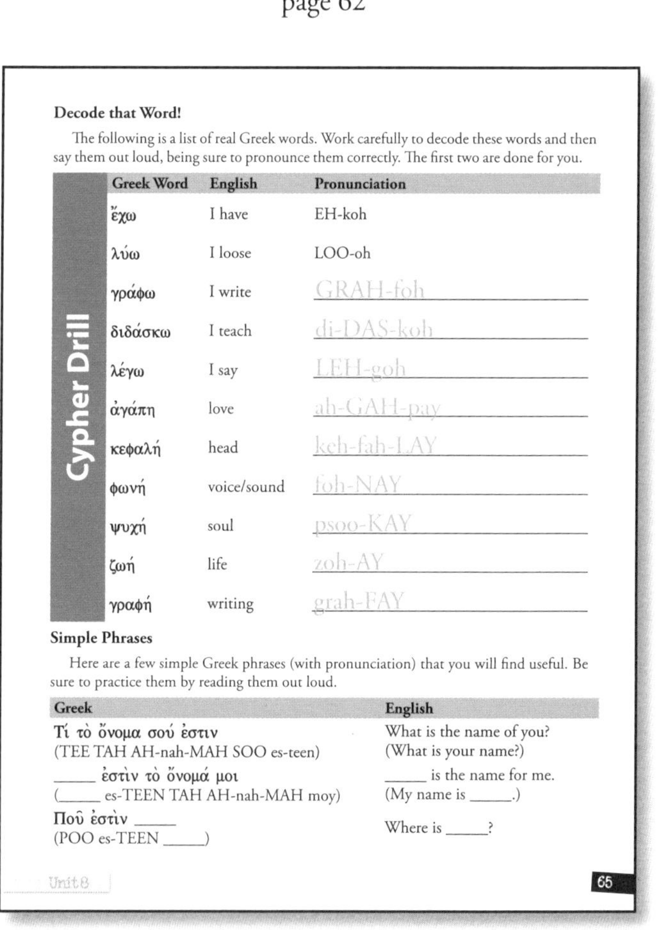

Decode that Word!

The following is a list of real Greek words. Work carefully to decode these words and then say them out loud, being sure to pronounce them correctly. The first two are done for you.

Cypher Drill

Greek Word	English	Pronunciation
ἔχω	I have	EH-koh
λύω	I loose	LOO-oh
γράφω	I write	GRAH-foh
διδάσκω	I teach	di-DAS-koh
λέγω	I say	LEH-goh
ἀγάπη	love	ah-GAH-pay
κεφαλή	head	keh-fah-LAY
φωνή	voice/sound	foh-NAY
ψυχή	soul	psoo-KAY
ζωή	life	zoh-AY
γραφή	writing	grah-FAY

Simple Phrases

Here are a few simple Greek phrases (with pronunciation) that you will find useful. Be sure to practice them by reading them out loud.

Greek	English
Τί τὸ ὄνομα σού ἐστιν (TEE TAH AH-nah-MAH SOO es-teen)	What is the name of you? (What is your name?)
_____ ἐστὶν τὸ ὄνομά μοι (_____ es-TEEN TAH AH-nah-MAH moy)	_____ is the name for me. (My name is _____.)
Ποῦ ἐστὶν _____ (POO es-TEEN _____)	Where is _____?

Unit 8 65

page 65

Use the clues listed to the right to unscramble each Greek-letter word and write the Greek letters in the correct blanks. Then write the letters marked with numbers in the matching numbered spaces below the puzzle to reveal a secret message. This message is the final clue in the Achilles Urn theft. Once you have decoded the secret message, write the thief's hiding spot in the space provided below.

Code Puzzle

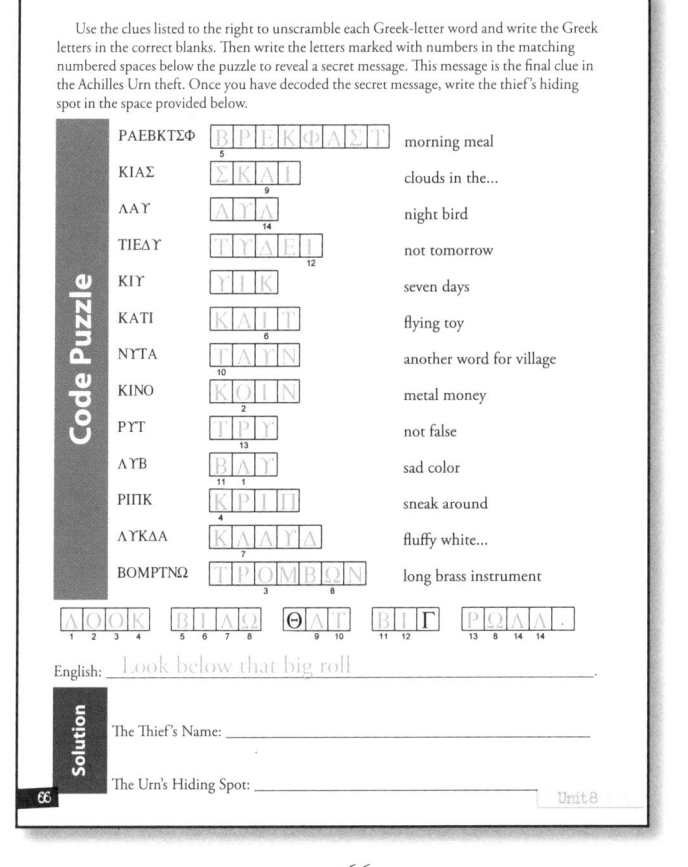

Scrambled	Answer	Clue
ΡΑΕΒΚΤΣΦ	ΒΡΕΚΦΑΣΤ	morning meal
ΚΙΑΣ	ΣΚΑΙ	clouds in the...
ΛΑΥ	ΑΥΛ	night bird
ΤΙΕΔΥ	ΤΥΔΕΙ	not tomorrow
ΚΙΥ	ΥΙΚ	seven days
ΚΑΤΙ	ΚΑΙΤ	flying toy
ΝΥΤΑ	ΤΑΥΝ	another word for village
ΚΙΝΟ	ΚΟΙΝ	metal money
ΡΥΤ	ΤΡΥ	not false
ΛΥΒ	ΒΛΥ	sad color
ΡΙΠΚ	ΚΡΙΠ	sneak around
ΛΥΚΔΑ	ΚΛΑΥΔ	fluffy white...
ΒΟΜΡΤΝΩ	ΤΡΟΜΒΩΝ	long brass instrument

ΛΟΟΚ ΒΙΛΩ ΘΑΤ ΒΙΓ ΡΩΛΛ.

English: Look below that big roll.

Solution

The Thief's Name: ______________________

The Urn's Hiding Spot: ______________________

66 Unit 8

page 66

The thief's escape route is mapped out above. After running all over town, he parked at the Burger Barn and hid the urn under the big hamburger roll on top of the roof, hoping to come back for it later.

Dr. Petri Diche was eliminated because he is not wearing a hat. Florence was eliminated because she is wearing glasses. Louie was eliminted because he is not wearing a watch. Rebecca was eliminated because she is not wearing boots. So, the thief must be Mr. Mini.

Notes

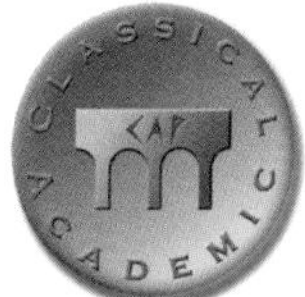
CLASSICAL
CAP
ACADEMIC

Notes

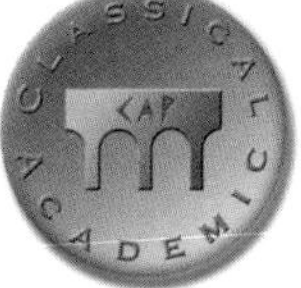
CLASSICAL
CAP
ACADEMIC

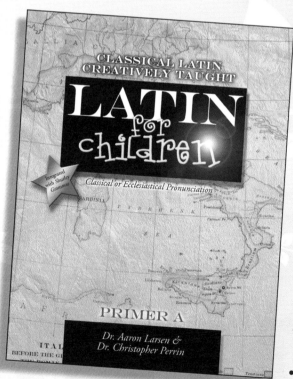

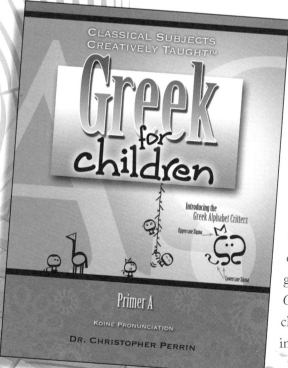